Gifts
Differing

GIFTS
DIFFERING

Understanding
Personality Type

Isabel Briggs Myers
With Peter B. Myers

CPP Books
Palo Alto, California
A Division of Consulting Psychologists Press, Inc.

96 95 94 93   10 9 8 7 6 5 4 3 2 1

Acknowledgments:

We thank the following researchers for granting permission to use their work as sources of figures in Gifts Differing: W. B. Stephens (1972)— Figures 16, 17, and 18; P. V. Miller (1965, 1967)—Figure 21; E. A. von Fange (1961)—Figure 23; and D. W. MacKinnon (1962)—Figure 33.

Library of Congress Cataloging-in-Publication Data

Myers, Isabel Briggs.
    Gifts differing: understanding personality type / Isabel Briggs Myers, with Peter B. Myers. --
        p.   cm.
    Originally published: Palo Alto, CA : Consulting Psychologists Press, 1990, c1980.
    Includes bibliographical references and index.
    ISBN: 0-89106-064-2
    1. Typology (Psychology) 2. Myers-Briggs Type Indicator.
I. Myers, Peter B. II. Title.
[BF698.3.M94 1993]
155.2'64--dc20   93-13087
                                      CIP

To all who desire to make fuller use of their gifts

For as we have many members in one body,
 and all members have not the same office:
So we, being many, are one body…
 and every one members one of another.

Having then gifts differing…

Rom. 12: 4–8

Contents

Publisher's Foreword   xiii

Preface   xvii

PART I

Theory

Chapter 1
An Orderly Reason for Personality Differences   1

Chapter 2
Extensions of Jung's Theory   17

PART II

Effects of the Preferences on Personality

Chapter 3
Type Tables for Comparison and Discovery   27

Chapter 4
Effect of the EI Preference   53

Chapter 5
Effect of the SN Preference   57

Chapter 6
Effect of the TF Preference   65

Chapter 7
Effect of the JP Preference   69

Chapter 8
Extraverted and Introverted Forms
of the Processes Compared   77

Chapter 9
Descriptions of the Sixteen Types   83

PART III

Practical Implications of Type

Chapter 10
Use of the Opposites   115

Chapter 11
Type and Marriage   123

Chapter 12
Type and Early Learning   131

Chapter 13
Learning Styles   139

Chapter 14
Type and Occupation   149

PART IV

Dynamics of Type Development

Chapter 15
Type and the Task of Growing Up   167

Chapter 16
Good Type Development   173

Chapter 17
Obstacles to Type Development   181

Chapter 18
Motivation for Type Development in Children   185

Chapter 19
Going On From Wherever You Are   191

Endnotes   203

References   205

Full-Size Type Table   208

Index   211

Publisher's Foreword

GIFTS DIFFERING IS a book about human personality—its richness, its diversity, its role in affecting career, marriage, and the meaning of life itself. It was written by a woman for whom the observation, study, and measurement of personality were consuming passions for more than half a century.

The conceptual framework by which Isabel Myers has organized her sensitive and optimistic observations is the typology of Carl Jung, slightly modified and elaborated by Myers and her mother, Katharine C. Briggs. Jung's theory, once mastered, provides a beautiful structure for understanding both similarities and differences among human beings.

Because a psychometric questionnaire called the *Myers-Briggs Type Indicator* is probably the simplest and most reliable method of determining a person's Jungian type, this book is also about the MBTI. Many of the insights into the role of personality in influencing human behavior have been developed from research with the MBTI and are reported in these pages.

The story behind the development of the MBTI is surely unique in the history of psychology. That story is the biography of a remarkable human being, or perhaps the saga of a whole family. It is instructive because it so clearly reveals the impact of parent on child and it is inspiring because it shows once more how much a single individual can achieve in the face of formidable obstacles.

The story begins with the marriage in 1896 of two unusually gifted people: Katharine Cook and Lyman Briggs.

Katharine, a thinker, a reader, a quiet observer, became intrigued with similarities and differences in human personality about the time of World War I. She began to develop her own typology, largely through the study of biography, and she then discovered that Jung had evolved a similar system, which she quickly accepted and began to explore and elaborate. Lyman was a versatile scientist when American science was in swaddling clothes, and he became a dominant figure during the first half of the twentieth century in establishing science as a crucial force in the halls of government. As director of the National Bureau of Standards, he played a role in the development of modern aviation and atomic energy and in the exploration of the stratosphere and of Antarctica. Although honored with numerous awards and memorialized by the establishment of Lyman Briggs College at Michigan State University (his alma mater), Dr. Briggs was remarkable for his modesty, humility, and compassion.

The Briggses had one child, Isabel, whom they educated at home except for a year or two in public school. Isabel Briggs entered Swarthmore College at age 17 and was graduated first in her class in 1919. At the end of her junior year, she married Clarence Myers. Until the outbreak of World War II, she functioned as a mother and homemaker, though she found time to publish two successful mystery novels, one of which won a prize over a story by Ellery Queen.

The suffering and tragedies of the war stirred Myers' desire to do something that might help people understand each other and avoid destructive conflicts. Having long since absorbed her mother's admiration of Jungian typology, she determined to devise a method of making the theory of practical use. Thus was born the idea of a "type indicator."

With no formal training in psychology or statistics, with no academic sponsorship or research grants, Myers began the painstaking task of developing an item pool that would tap the attitudes, feelings, perceptions, and behaviors of the different psychological types as she and her mother had come to understand them. Her adolescent children and their classmates were early guinea pigs, but anyone whose type Myers could judge was apt to be asked to contribute ideas or to respond to items.

An habitual reader, she haunted libraries to teach herself what she needed to know of statistics and psychometrics. She apprenticed herself to Edward N. Hay, who later founded one of the first successful personnel consulting firms in the United States. She persuaded countless school principals in eastern Pennsylvania to allow her to test their students. And she spent many a long evening scoring questions and tabulating data.

For the first decade or so of this work, Myers received little external reinforcement, except from members of her family. Through her father, she met a medical school dean who allowed her to test his students, an entrée that she expanded through the years until she had MBTI results for more than 5,000 medical students and 10,000 nurses.

The response to Myers' efforts from organized psychology was certainly cool if not hostile. In the first place, the measurement of personality was considered a dubious enterprise by many psychologists. Furthermore, among those few who were interested in personality theory and measurement, typologies were not in good repute. Trait and factor scales were the focus of research and surely Myers' lack of establishment credentials did not help the MBTI to win acceptance. There is no evidence that Myers was in the least daunted by either the skeptics or the critics. Throughout the 1950s and 1960s, she continued to corner principals and deans in their offices and extract agreements for administering the MBTI.

Myers's work did attract favorable attention from a few assessment experts. When Henry Chauncey, the thoughtful head of Educational Testing Service (ETS), became aware of the MBTI, he was eager to learn more about it. In due course, this led to a contract between Myers and ETS to publish and market the MBTI. Not everyone at ETS shared Chauncey's enthusiasm. Except for the development of Forms E and F, and the publication of a manual in 1962, the MBTI did not experience further development under ETS auspices. Donald T. MacKinnon, the distinguished director of the Institute of Personality Assessment and Research at the University of California, added the MBTI to the tests used in assessing creative persons and published supportive findings. Professor Harold Grant of Michigan State and Auburn Universities and Dr. Mary McCaulley of the University of Florida also undertook significant research with the instrument.

In 1975 publication of the MBTI was transferred to Consulting Psychologists Press, and the Center for Applications of Psychological Type was organized as a service and research laboratory for the inventory. Recent years have seen the establishment of a journal of research and the formation of an association of users of the MBTI. Such widespread acceptance might have persuaded most researchers past age 75 to lay down their calculators and pencils, but not Isabel Myers. At the age of 82 she was at work on a revised manual for the MBTI, and she corrected the proofs for *Gifts Differing* long after she was profoundly weakened by her final illness.

Although it was already apparent during Myers' last years that the MBTI would probably become the most widely used personality measure for nonpsychiatric populations, Myers never showed the degree of vanity or conceit such an achievement might warrant: She remained pleased, grateful, and ever enthusiastic about the usefulness of the inventory. Nor was there ever a hint of bitterness for all the years of condescension and rejection.

These characteristic attitudes of Isabel Myers will be apparent in the pages that follow. Her focus throughout this book is on the beauty, the strength, the infinite possibilities of human personality in all its fascinating varieties. She would probably not argue for the perfectibility of the human species, but through all the painful and disillusioning events of the past four decades, Myers retained a touching faith in people and a refreshing optimism about humanity, which make *Gifts Differing* much more than an important treatise on the *Myers-Briggs Type Indicator*. We are happy to be able to bring it to you.

JOHN D. BLACK
July 1980

Preface

THIS BOOK IS written in the belief that many problems might be dealt with more successfully if approached in the light of C. G. Jung's theory of psychological types. The first English translation of his *Psychological Types* was published by Harcourt Brace in 1923. My mother, Katharine C. Briggs, introduced it into our family and made it a part of our lives. She and I waited a long time for someone to devise an instrument that would reflect not only one's preference for extraversion or introversion but one's preferred kind of perception and judgment as well. In the summer of 1942 we undertook to do it ourselves. Since then the *Myers-Briggs Type Indicator* has yielded a wide range of information about the practical bearings of type.

The implications of the theory, however, go beyond statistics and can be expressed only in human terms. *Gifts Differing* presents an informal account of type and its consequences as they have appeared to us over the years. In this material I hope parents, teachers, students, counselors, clinicians, clergy—and all others who are concerned with the realization of human potential—may find a rationale for many of the personality differences they encounter in their work

It has taken three generations to make this book: the deep insight of my mother's (INFJ) introverted intuition into the meaning of type; my own (INFP) introverted-feeling conviction about the importance of type's practical applications; and my (ENFP) son Peter's invaluable combination of extravert viewpoint, intuitive drive, gift of expression, and sense of priorities—without which these pages might never have been finished.

ISABEL BRIGGS MYERS
July 1980

PART I

Theory

CHAPTER 1

An Orderly Reason for Personality Differences

IT IS FASHIONABLE to say that the individual is unique. Each is the product of his or her own heredity and environment and, therefore, is different from everyone else. From a practical standpoint, however, the doctrine of uniqueness is not useful without an exhaustive case study of every person to be educated or counseled or understood. Yet we cannot safely assume that other people's minds work on the same principles as our own. All too often, others with whom we come in contact do not reason as we reason, or do not value the things we value, or are not interested in what interests us.

The merit of the theory presented here is that it enables us to expect specific personality differences in particular people and to cope with the people and the differences in a constructive way. Briefly, the theory is that much seemingly chance variation in human behavior is not due to chance; it is in fact the logical result of a few basic, observable differences in mental functioning.

These basic differences concern the way people *prefer* to use their minds, specifically, the way they perceive and the way they make judgments. *Perceiving* is here understood to include the processes of becoming aware of things, people, occurrences, and ideas. *Judging* includes the processes of coming to conclusions about what has been perceived. Together, perception and judgment, which make up a large portion of people's total mental activity, govern much of their outer behavior, because perception—by definition—determines what people see in a situation, and their judgment determines what they decide to do about it. Thus, it is reasonable that basic differences in perception or judgment should result in corresponding differences in behavior.

1

Two Ways of Perceiving

As Jung points out in *Psychological Types*, humankind is equipped with two distinct and sharply contrasting ways of perceiving. One means of perception is the familiar process of sensing, by which we become aware of things directly through our five senses. The other is the process of *intuition*, which is indirect perception by way of the unconscious, incorporating ideas or associations that the unconscious tacks on to perceptions coming from outside. These unconscious contributions range from the merest masculine "hunch" or "woman's intuition" to the crowning examples of creative art or scientific discovery.

The existence of distinct ways of perceiving would seem self-evident. People perceive through their senses, and they also perceive things that are not and never have been present to their senses. The theory adds the suggestion that the two kinds of perception compete for a person's attention and that most people, from infancy up, *enjoy* one more than the other. When people prefer sensing, they are so interested in the actuality around them that they have little attention to spare for ideas coming faintly out of nowhere. Those people who prefer intuition are so engrossed in pursuing the possibilities it presents that they seldom look very intently at the actualities. For instance, readers who prefer sensing will tend to confine their attention to what is said here on the page. Readers who prefer intuition are likely to read between and beyond the lines to the possibilities that come to mind.

As soon as children exercise a preference between the two ways of perceiving, a basic difference in development begins. The children have enough command of their mental processes to be able to use the favorite processes more often and to neglect the processes they enjoy less. Whichever process they prefer, whether sensing or intuition, they will use more, paying closer attention to its stream of impressions and fashioning their idea of the world from what the process reveals. The other kind of perception will be background, a little out of focus.

With the advantage of constant practice, the preferred process grows more controlled and more trustworthy. The children become more adult in their use of the preferred process than in their less frequent use of the neglected one. Their enjoyment extends from the process itself to activities requiring the process, and they tend to develop the surface traits that result from looking at life in a particular way.

Thus, by a natural sequence of events, the child who prefers sensing and the child who prefers intuition develop along divergent lines. Each becomes relatively adult in an area where the other remains relatively childlike. Both channel their interests and energy into activities that give them a chance to use their mind the way they prefer. Both acquire a set of surface traits that grows out of the basic preferences beneath. This is the SN preference: S for sensing and N for intuition.

Two Ways of Judging

A basic difference in judgment arises from the existence of two distinct and sharply contrasting ways of coming to conclusions. One way is by the use of *thinking,* that is, by a logical process, aimed at an impersonal finding. The other is by *feeling,* that is, by appreciation—equally reasonable in its fashion—bestowing on things a personal, subjective value.

These two ways of judging would also seem self-evident. Most people would agree that they make some decisions with thinking and some with feeling, and that the two methods do not always reach the same result from a given set of facts. The theory suggests that a person is almost certain to enjoy and trust one way of judging more than the other. In judging the ideas presented here, a reader who considers first whether they are consistent and logical is using thinking judgment. A reader who is conscious first that the ideas are pleasing or displeasing, supporting or threatening ideas already prized, is using feeling judgment.

Whichever judging process a child prefers he or she will use more often, trust more implicitly, and be much more ready to obey. The other kind of judgment will be a sort of minority opinion, half-heard and often wholly disregarded.

Thus, the child who prefers thinking develops along divergent lines from the child who prefers feeling, even when both like the same perceptive process and start with the same perceptions. Both are happier and more effective in activities that call for the sort of judgments that they are better equipped to make. The child who prefers feeling becomes more adult in the handling of human relationships. The child who prefers thinking grows more adept in the organization of facts and ideas. Their basic preference for the personal or the impersonal approach to life results in distinguishing surface traits. This is the TF preference: T for thinking and F for feeling.

Combinations of Perception and Judgment

The TF preference (thinking or feeling) is entirely independent of the SN preference (sensing or intuition). Either kind of judgment can team up with either kind of perception. Thus, four combinations occur:

ST	Sensing plus thinking
SF	Sensing plus feeling
NF	Intuition plus feeling
NT	Intuition plus thinking

Each of these combinations produces a different kind of personality, characterized by the *interests, values, needs, habits of mind, and surface traits that naturally result* from the combination. Combinations with a common preference will share some qualities, but each combination has qualities all its own, arising from the *interaction* of the preferred way of looking at life and the preferred way of judging what is seen.

Whatever a person's particular combination of preferences may be, others with the same combination are apt to be the easiest to understand and like. They will tend to have similar interests, since they share the same kind of perception, and to consider the same things important, since they share the same kind of judgment.

On the other hand, people who differ on both preferences will be hard to understand and hard to predict—except that on every debatable question they are likely to take opposite stands. If these very opposite people are merely acquaintances, the clash of views may not matter, but if they are co-workers, close associates, or members of the same family, the constant opposition can be a strain.

Many destructive conflicts arise simply because two people are using opposite kinds of perception and judgment. When the origin of such a conflict is recognized, it becomes less annoying and easier to handle.

An even more destructive conflict may exist between people and their jobs, when the job makes no use of the worker's natural combination of perception and judgment but constantly demands the opposite combination.

The following paragraphs sketch the contrasting personalities that are expected in theory and found in practice to result from each of the four possible combinations of perception and judgment.

Sensing Plus Thinking

The ST (sensing plus thinking) people rely primarily on sensing for purposes of perception and on thinking for purposes of judgment. Thus, their main interest focuses upon facts, because facts can be collected and verified directly by the senses—by seeing, hearing, touching, counting, weighing, measuring. ST people approach their decisions regarding these facts by impersonal analysis, because of their trust in thinking, with its step-by-step logical process of reasoning from cause to effect, from premise to conclusion.

In consequence, their personalities tend to be practical and matter-of-fact, and their best chances of success and satisfaction lie in fields that demand impersonal analysis of concrete facts, such as economics, law, surgery, business, accounting, production, and the handling of machines and materials.

Sensing Plus Feeling

The SF (sensing plus feeling) people, too, rely primarily on sensing for purposes of perception, but they prefer feeling for purposes of judgment. They approach their decisions with personal warmth because their feeling weighs how much things matter to themselves and others.

They are more interested in facts about people than in facts about things and, therefore, they tend to be sociable and friendly. They are most likely to succeed and be satisfied in work where their personal warmth can be applied effectively to the immediate situation, as in pediatrics, nursing, teaching (especially elementary), social work, selling of tangibles, and service-with-a-smile jobs.

Intuition Plus Feeling

The NF (intuition plus feeling) people possess the same personal warmth as SF people because of their shared use of feeling for purposes of judgment, but because the NFs prefer intuition to sensing, they do not center their attention upon the concrete situation. Instead they focus on possibilities, such as new projects (things that haven't ever happened but might be made to happen) or new truths (things that are not yet known but might be found out). The new project or the new truth is imagined by the unconscious processes and then intuitively perceived as an idea that feels like an inspiration.

The personal warmth and commitment with which the NF people seek and follow up a possibility are impressive. They are both enthusiastic and insightful. Often they have a marked gift of language and can communicate both the possibility they see and the value they attach to it. They are most likely to find success and satisfaction in work that calls for creativity to meet a human need. They may excel in teaching (particularly college and high school), preaching, advertising, selling of intangibles, counseling, clinical psychology, psychiatry, writing, and most fields of research.

Intuition Plus Thinking

The NT (intuition plus thinking) people also use intuition but team it with thinking. Although they focus on a possibility, they approach it with impersonal analysis. Often they choose a theoretical or executive possibility and subordinate the human element.

NTs tend to be logical and ingenious and are most successful in solving problems in a field of special interest, whether scientific research, electronic computing, mathematics, the more complex aspects of finance, or any sort of development or pioneering in technical areas.

Everyone has probably met all four kinds of people: ST people, who are practical and matter-of-fact; the sympathetic and friendly SF people; NF people, who are characterized by their enthusiasm and insight; and NT people, who are logical and ingenious.

The skeptic may ask how four apparently basic categories of people could have gone unnoticed in the past. The answer is that the categories *have* been noted repeatedly and by different investigators or theorists.

Vernon (1938) cited three systems of classification derived by different methods but which are strikingly parallel. Each reflects the combinations of perception and judgment: Thurstone (1931), by factor analysis of vocational interest scores, found four main factors corresponding to interest in business, in people, in language, and in science; Gundlach and Gerum (1931), from inspection of interest intercorrelations, deduced five main "types of ability," namely, technical, social, creative, and intellectual, plus physical skill; Spranger (1928), from logical and intuitive considerations, derived six "types of men," namely, economic, social, religious, and theoretical, plus aesthetic and political.

The Extraversion-Introversion
Preference

Another basic difference in people's use of perception and judgment arises from their relative interest in their outer and inner worlds. *Introversion*, in the sense given to it by Jung in formulating the term and the idea, is one of two complementary orientations to life; its complement is *extraversion*. The introvert's main interests are in the inner world of concepts and ideas, while the extravert is more involved with the outer world of people and things. Therefore, when circumstances permit, the introvert concentrates perception and judgment upon ideas, while the extravert likes to focus them on the outside environment.

This is not to say that anyone is limited either to the inner world or to the outer. Well-developed introverts can deal ably with the world around them when necessary, but they do their best work inside their heads, in reflection. Similarly well-developed extraverts can deal effectively with ideas, but they do their best work externally, in action. For both kinds, the natural preference remains, like right- or left-handedness.

For example, some readers, who would like to get to the practical applications of this theory, are looking at it from the extravert standpoint. Other readers, who feel more interest in the insight that the theory may provide for understanding themselves and human nature in general, are seeing it from the introvert point of view.

Since the EI preference (extraversion or introversion) is completely independent of the SN and TF preferences, extraverts and introverts may have any of the four combinations of perception and judgment. For example, among the STs, the introverts (IST) organize the facts and principles related to a situation; this approach is useful in economics or law. The extraverts (EST) organize the situation itself, including any idle bystanders, and get things rolling, which is useful in business and industry. Things usually move faster for the extraverts; things move in a more considered direction for the introverts.

Among the NF people, the introverts (INF) work out their insights slowly and carefully, searching for eternal verities. The extraverts (ENF) have an urge to communicate and put their inspirations into practice. If the extraverts' results are more extensive, the introverts' may be more profound.

The Judgment-Perception
Preference

One more preference enters into the identification of type—the choice between the *perceptive* attitude and the *judging* attitude as a way of life, a method of dealing with the world around us. Although people must of course use both perception and judgment, both cannot be used at the same moment. So people shift back and forth between the perceptive and judging attitudes, sometimes quite abruptly, as when a parent with a high tolerance for children's noise suddenly decides that enough is enough.

There is a time to perceive and a time to judge, and many times when either attitude might be appropriate. Most people find one attitude more comfortable than the other, feel more at home in it, and use it as often as possible in dealing with the outer world. For example, some readers are still following this explanation with an open mind; they are, at least for the moment, using perception. Other readers have decided by now that they agree or disagree; they are using judgment.

There is a fundamental opposition between the two attitudes. In order to come to a conclusion, people use the judging attitude and have to shut off perception for the time being. All the evidence is in, and anything more is irrelevant and immaterial. The time has come to arrive at a verdict. Conversely, in the perceptive attitude people shut off judgment. Not all the evidence is in; new developments will occur. It is much too soon to do anything irrevocable.

This preference makes the difference between the judging people, who order their lives, and the perceptive people, who just live them. Both attitudes have merit. Either can make a satisfying way of life, if a person can switch temporarily to the opposite attitude when it is really needed.

Summary of the Four Preferences

Under the theory presented here, personality is structured by four preferences concerning the use of perception and judgment. Each of these preferences is a fork in the road of human development and determines which of two contrasting forms of excellence a person will pursue. How much excellence people actually achieve depends in part on their energy and their aspirations, but according to type theory, *the kind of excellence toward which they are headed* is determined by the inborn preferences that direct them at each fork in the road.

Preference for		Affects a person's choice
EI	Extraversion or Introversion	To focus the dominant (favorite) process on the outer world or on the world of ideas
SN	Sensing or Intuition	To use one kind of perception instead of the other when either could be used
TF	Thinking or Feeling	To use one kind of judgment instead of the other when either could be used
JP	Judgment or Perception	To use the judging or the perceptive attitude for dealing with the outer world

Creation of "Type" by Exercise of the Preferences

Under this theory, people create their "type" through exercise of their individual preferences regarding perception and judgment. The interests, values, needs, and habits of mind that naturally result from any set of preferences tend to produce a recognizable set of traits and potentialities.

Individuals can, therefore, be described in part by stating their four preferences, such as ENTP. Such a person can be expected to be different from others in ways characteristic of his or her type. To describe people as ENTPs does not infringe on their right to self-determination: They have already exercised this right by preferring E and N and T and P. Identifying and remembering people's types shows respect not only for their abstract right to develop along lines of their own choosing, but also for the concrete ways in which they are and prefer to be different from others.

The Role of the Dominant Process

It is easier to recognize a person's preferred way of perception and way of judging than it is to tell which of the two is the dominant process. There is no doubt that a ship needs a captain with undisputed authority to set its course and bring it safely to the desired port. It would never make harbor if each person at the helm in turn aimed at a different destination and altered course accordingly.

In the same way, people need some governing force in their make-up. They need to develop their best process to the point where it dominates and unifies their lives. In the natural course of events, each person does just that.

For example, those ENTs who find intuition more interesting than thinking will naturally give intuition the right of way and subordinate thinking to it. Their intuition acquires an unquestioned personal validity that no other process can approach. They will enjoy, use, and trust it most. Their lives will be so shaped as to give maximum freedom for the pursuit of intuitive goals. Because intuition is a perceptive process, these ENTs will deal with the world in the perceptive attitude, which makes them ENTPs.

They will consult their judgment, their thinking, only when it does not conflict with their intuition. Even then, they will use it only to a degree, depending on how well developed it is. They may make fine use of thinking in pursuit of something they want because of their intuition, but ENTPs will not permit thinking to reject what they are pursuing.

On the other hand, those ENTs who find thinking more attractive than intuition will tend to let their thinking take charge of their lives, with intuition in second place. Thinking will dictate the goals, and intuition will only be allowed to suggest suitable means of reaching them. Since the process they prefer is a judging one, these ENTs will deal with the world in the judging attitude; therefore they are ENTJs.

Similarly, some ESFs find more satisfaction in feeling than in sensing; they let their feeling take charge of their lives, with sensing in second place. Feeling is then supreme and unquestioned. In any conflict with the other processes, feeling dominates. The lives of these ESFs will be shaped to serve their feeling values. Because of the preference for feeling, a judging process, they will deal with the world in the judging attitude. They are ESFJ.

ESFJs will pay real attention to their perception, their sensing, only when it is in accord with their feeling. Even then, they will respect it only to a degree, depending on how well they have developed it. They will not acknowledge doubts raised by the senses concerning something valued by their feeling.

However, other ESFs find sensing more rewarding than feeling and will tend to put sensing first and feeling in second place. Their lives will be shaped to serve their sensing—to provide a stream of experiences that provide something interesting to see, hear, taste, or handle. Feeling will be allowed to contribute but not to interfere. Because sensing, a perceptive process, is preferred, these ESFs will deal with the world in the perceptive attitude, and therefore they are ESFPs.

This phenomenon, of the dominant process overshadowing the other processes and shaping the personality accordingly, was empirically noted by Jung in the course of his work and became, along with the extraversion-introversion preference, the basis of his *Psychological Types*.

Some people dislike the idea of a dominant process and prefer to think of themselves as using all four processes equally. However, Jung holds that such impartiality, where it actually exists, keeps all of the processes relatively undeveloped and produces a "primitive mentality," because opposite ways of doing the same thing interfere with each other if neither has priority. If one perceptive process is to reach a high degree of development, it needs undivided attention much of the time, which means that the other must be shut off frequently and will be less developed. If one judging process is to become highly developed, it must similarly have the right of way. One perceptive process and one judging process can develop side by side, provided one is used in the service of the other. But one process—sensing, intuition, thinking, or feeling—must have clear sovereignty, with opportunity to reach its full development, if a person is to be really effective.

The Role of the Auxiliary Process

One process alone, however, is not enough. For people to be balanced, they need adequate (but by no means equal) development of a second process, not as a rival to the dominant process but as a welcome auxiliary. If the dominant process is a judging one, the auxiliary process will be perceptive: Either sensing or intuition can supply sound material for judgments. If the dominant process is perceptive, the auxiliary process will be a judging one: Either thinking or feeling can give continuity of aim.

If a person has no useful development of an auxiliary process, the absence is likely to be obvious. An extreme perceptive with no judgment is all sail and no rudder. An extreme judging type with no perception is all form and no content.

In addition to supplementing the dominant process in its main field of activity, the auxiliary has another responsibility. It carries the main burden of supplying adequate balance (but not equality) between extraversion and introversion, between the outer and inner worlds. For all types, the dominant process becomes deeply absorbed in the world that interests them most, and such absorption is fitting and proper. The world of their choice is not only more interesting, it is more important to them. It is where they can do their best work and function at their best level, and it lays claim to the almost undivided attention of their best process. If the dominant process becomes deeply involved in less important matters, the main business of life will suffer. In general, therefore, the less important matters are left to the auxiliary process.

For extraverts, the dominant process *is* concerned with the outer world of people and things, and the auxiliary process has to look after their inner lives, without which the extraverts would be extreme in the extraversion and, in the opinions of their better-balanced associates, superficial.

Introverts have less choice about participating in both worlds. The outer life is thrust upon them whether they want one or not. Their dominant process is engrossed with the inner world of ideas, and the auxiliary process does what it can about their outer lives. In effect, the dominant process says to the auxiliary, "Go out there and tend to the things that can't be avoided, and don't ask me to work on them except when it's absolutely necessary."

Introverts are reluctant to use the dominant process on the outer world any more than necessary because of the predictable results. If the dominant process, which is the most adult and conscientious process, is used on outer things, it will involve the introverts in more extraversion than they can handle, and such involvement will cost them privacy and peace.

The success of introverts' contacts with the outer world depends on the effectiveness of their auxiliary. If their auxiliary process is not adequately developed, their outer lives will be very awkward, accidental, and uncomfortable. Thus there is a more obvious penalty upon introverts who fail to develop a useful auxiliary than upon the extraverts with a like deficiency.

Difficulty of Seeing the
Introverts' Dominant Process

In the extraverts, the dominant process, being extraverted, is not only visible but conspicuous. Their most trusted, most skilled, most adult way of using their minds is devoted to the outside world. Therefore it is the side ordinarily presented, the side others see, even in casual contacts. The extraverts' best process tends to be immediately apparent.

With introverts, the reverse is true. The dominant process is habitually and stubbornly introverted; when their attention must turn to the outer world, they tend to use the auxiliary process. Except for those who are very close to introverts, or very much interested in work that they love (which is probably the best way of getting close to them), people are not likely to be admitted to the introverts' inner worlds. Most people see only the side introverts present to the outer world, which is mostly their auxiliary process, their second best.

The result is a paradox. Introverts whose dominant process is a judging process, either thinking or feeling, do not *outwardly* act like judging people. What shows on the outside is the perceptiveness of their auxiliary process, and they live their outer lives mainly in the perceptive attitude. The inner judgingness is not apparent until something comes up that is important to their inner worlds. At such moments they may take a startlingly positive stand.

Similarly, introverts whose dominant process is perceptive, either sensing or intuition, do not outwardly behave like perceptive people. They show the judgingness of the auxiliary process and live their outer lives mainly in the judging attitude.

A good way to visualize the difference is to think of the dominant process as the General and the auxiliary process as his Aide. In the case of the extravert, the General is always out in the open. Other people meet him immediately and do their business directly with him. They can get the official viewpoint on anything at any time. The Aide stands respectfully in the background or disappears inside the tent. The introvert's General is inside the tent, working on matters of top priority. The Aide is outside fending off interruptions, or, if he is inside helping the General, he comes out to see what is wanted. It is the Aide whom others meet and with whom they do their business. Only when the business is very important (or the friendship is very close) do others get in to see the General himself.

If people do not realize that there *is* a General in the tent who far outranks the Aide they have met, they may easily assume that the Aide is in sole charge. This is a regrettable mistake. It leads not only to an underestimation of the introvert's abilities but also to an incomplete understanding of his wishes, plans, and point of view. The only source for such inside information is the General.

A cardinal precaution in dealing with introverts, therefore, is not to assume, just from ordinary contact, that they have revealed what really matters to them. Whenever there is a decision to be made that involves introverts, they should be told about it as fully as possible. If the matter is important to them, the General will come out of the tent and reveal a number of new things, and the ultimate decision will have a better chance of being right.

Finding Which Process
Is Dominant

There are three ways of deducing the dominant process from the four letters of a person's type. The dominant process must, of course, be either the preferred perceptive process (as shown by the second letter) or the preferred judging process (as shown by the third).

The JP preference can be used to determine the dominant process, but must be used differently with extraverts and introverts. JP reflects only the process used in *dealing with the outside world.* As explained earlier, the extravert's dominant process prefers the outer world. Hence the extravert's dominant process shows on the JP preference. If an extravert's type ends in J, the dominant process is a judging one, either T or F. If the type ends in P, the dominant process is a perceptive one, either S or N.

For introverts, the exact opposite is true. The introvert's dominant process does *not* show on the JP preference, because introverts prefer not to use the dominant process in dealing with the outer world. The J or P in their type therefore reflects the *auxiliary* instead of the dominant process. If an introvert's type ends in J, the dominant process is a perceptive one, S or N. If the type ends in P, the dominant process is a judging one, T or F.

For ready reference, the underlined letters in Figure 1 indicate the dominant process for each of the sixteen types.

Figure 1. The Dominant Process of Each Type

	ST	SF	NF	NT
I – – J	IS̲TJ	IS̲FJ	IN̲FJ	IN̲TJ
I – – P	IST̲P	ISF̲P	INF̲P	INT̲P
E – – P	ES̲TP	ES̲FP	EN̲FP	EN̲TP
E – – J	EST̲J	ESF̲J	ENF̲J	ENT̲J

	Extravert	Introvert
The JP preference shows how a person prefers to deal with the _____ world.	outer	outer
The _____ process shows up on the JP preference.	dominant	auxiliary
The dominant process is used in the _____ world.	outer	inner
The auxiliary process is used in the _____ world.	inner	outer

CHAPTER 2

Extensions of Jung's Theory

CHAPTER 1 PRESENTS the type theory in a less abstruse form than Jung employed in his *Psychological Types* and states the theory in terms of the everyday aspects seen in well-balanced people. In addition to their dominant process, such people have an auxiliary developed well enough to provide a balance between judgment and perception *and* between extraversion *and* introversion. Nowhere in Jung's book does he describe these normal, balanced types with an auxiliary process at their disposal. He portrays each process in sharpest focus and with maximum contrast between its extraverted and introverted forms; consequently, he describes the rare, theoretically "pure" types, who have little or no development of the auxiliary.

Jung's approach has several unfortunate effects. By ignoring the auxiliary, he bypasses the combinations of perception and judgment and their broad categories of interest in business, people, language, and science. The results of these combinations—the everyday forms in which the types are met—are dismissed in seven lines on page 515 (see page 19 of this book). Consequently, other researchers, who have reinvented the categories under different names, were unaware of the parallels between their findings and Jung's theories.

Another serious result of ignoring the auxiliary process is the distorted descriptions of the individual introvert types. These types depend on the auxiliary for their extraversion, that is, for their outer personalities, their communication with the world, and their means of taking action. To portray them with no auxiliary is to portray them with no extraversion—unable to communicate, to use their insights, or to have any impact on the outer world.

In view of Jung's deep appreciation of the introverts' value, it is ironical that he lets his passion for the abstract betray him into concentrating on cases of "pure" introversion. He not only describes people with no extraversion at all, but seems to present them as typical of introverts in general. By failing to convey that introverts with a good auxiliary *are* effective and play an indispensable part in the world, he opens the door for a general misunderstanding of his theory. Many people so completely misunderstood it that they took the basic extravert-introvert difference to be a difference in adjustment instead of a legitimate choice of orientation.

Few of Jung's readers appear to have realized that his type concepts had a bearing on the familiar daily problems of educating people, counseling them, employing them, communicating with them, and living in the same family with them. For decades, therefore, the practical utility of his theory went unexplored.

Overlooked Implications of Jung's Theory

To be useful, a personality theory must portray *and explain* people as they are. Jung's theory must, therefore, be extended to include the following three essentials.

Constant Presence of the Auxiliary Process

The first requisite for balance is development of the auxiliary process in support of the dominant process. Jung does not mention the auxiliary process in *Psychological Types* until page 513, after all his descriptions of the types.

- In the foregoing descriptions I have no desire to give my readers the impression that such pure types occur at all frequently in actual practice. (1923, p. 513)

- In conjunction with the most differentiated function, another function of secondary importance, and therefore of inferior differentiation in consciousness, is constantly present, and is a relatively determining factor. (1923, p. 513)

- Experience shows that the secondary function is always one whose nature is different from, though not antagonistic to, the leading function: Thus, for example, thinking, as primary function, can readily pair with intuition as auxiliary, or indeed equally well with sensation, but...never with feeling. (1923, p. 515)

Results of the Combinations of Perception and Judgment

The characteristics that result from these combinations, as outlined in Chapter 1, provide perhaps the most easily recognized aspect of type. All Jung writes about them is the following:

> From these combinations well-known pictures arise, the practical intellect for instance paired with sensation, the speculative intellect breaking through with intuition, the artistic intuition which selects and presents its images by means of feeling judgment, the philosophical intuition which, in league with a vigorous intellect, translates its vision into the sphere of comprehensible thought, and so forth. (1923, p. 515)

Role of the Auxiliary in Balancing Extraversion-Introversion

The basic principle that the auxiliary provides needed extraversion for the introverts and needed introversion for the extraverts is vitally important. The extraverts' auxiliary gives them access to their own inner life and to the world of ideas; the introverts' auxiliary gives them a means to adapt to the world of action and to deal with it effectively.

Jung's only allusions to this fact are cryptically brief. As a result, almost all his followers except van der Hoop seem to miss the principle involved. They assume that the *two* most developed processes are used in the favorite sphere (both extraverted or both introverted) and that the other sphere is left to the mercy of the two inferior processes. Jung writes:

> For all the types appearing in practice, the principle holds good that besides the conscious main function there is also a relatively unconscious, auxiliary function which is in every respect different from the nature of the main function. (1923, p. 515)

The operative words are "in every respect." If the auxiliary process differs from the dominant process in every respect, it *cannot* be introverted where the dominant process is introverted. It has to be extraverted if the dominant process is introverted, and introverted if the dominant process is extraverted.[1] This interpretation is confirmed by Jung in two other sentences, the first about the introvert thinker, the second about the extravert.

The relatively unconscious functions of feeling,
intuition and sensation, which counterbalance
introverted thinking, are inferior in quality and have
a primitive, extraverted character. (1923, p. 489)

When the mechanism of extraversion predominates…
the most highly differentiated function has a constantly
extraverted application, while the inferior functions are
found in the service of introversion. (1923, p. 426)[2]

The conclusion that the auxiliary process takes care of the extraversion of the introvert and the introversion of the extravert is confirmed by observation. In any well-balanced introvert, the observer can *see* that the extraverting is carried on by the auxiliary process. For example, ISTJ people (introverted sensing types preferring thinking to feeling as auxiliary) normally run their outer life with their second-best process, thinking, so it is conducted with impersonal system and order. They do *not* leave it to their third-best process, feeling, as they would have to do if both their sensing and their thinking were introverted. Similarly, INFP people (introverted feeling types preferring intuition to sensing as auxiliary) normally run their outer life with their second-best process, their intuition, so their outer life is characterized by spurts and projects and enthusiasm. They do *not* leave it to their third-best process, sensing, as they would have to do if both their feeling and their intuition were introverted.

A more subtle kind of evidence lies in the "extraverted character" of the introvert's auxiliary process. For example, in a well-balanced ISTJ the observable auxiliary process, thinking, can be seen to resemble the thinking of the extraverted thinker more than that of the introverted thinker. This point can be tested with any introvert by comparing the auxiliary process with Chapter 8, Figures 28–31, where the differences between extraverted and introverted thinking, extraverted and introverted feeling, etc., are shown.

Good type development thus demands that the auxiliary supplement the dominant process in two respects. It must supply a useful degree of balance not only between perception and judgment but *also between extraversion and introversion*. When it fails to do so it leaves the individual literally "unbalanced," retreating into the preferred world and consciously or unconsciously afraid of the other world. Such cases do occur and may seem to support the widespread assumption among Jungian analysts that the dominant and auxiliary are naturally both extraverted or both introverted; but such cases are not the norm: They are instances of insufficient use and development of the auxiliary. To live happily and effectively in both worlds, people need a *balancing* auxiliary that will make it possible to adapt in both directions—to the world around them and to their inner selves.

The Resulting Sixteen Types

When the auxiliary process is taken into consideration, it splits each of Jung's types into two. Instead of merely the introverted thinker, there are the introverted thinker with sensing and the introverted thinker with intuition. Thus there are sixteen types in place of Jung's eight. Sixteen would be an unwieldy number to keep in mind if the types were arbitrary, unrelated categories, but each is the logical result of its own preferences and is closely related to other types that share some of those preferences. (The relationships can be visualized logically and easily through familiarity with the Type Table in Chapter 3, Figure 2.)

To attempt to determine a person's type by observation, it is unnecessary to consider all sixteen possibilities at once. Any preference that seems reasonably certain will reduce the possibilities by half. For example, any introvert belongs to one of the eight introvert types. An intuitive introvert belongs to one of the four IN types. If such a person prefers thinking to feeling, the type is refined further to INT. The final step, identification of the dominant process, will depend on the JP preference.

The Role of the Judgment-Perception Preference

The JP preference completes the structure of type. As explained at the end of Chapter 1, this preference is indispensable for ascertaining which process is dominant. Students of Jung will not, however, find any reference to the JP preference in *Psychological Types*. Although he occasionally refers to judging and perceptive types among extraverts, Jung never mentions that the JP difference can be seen in introverts and that it reflects the character of their extraversion. This omission is inevitable because he never discusses the introvert's extraversion.

Instead, Jung divides the types into rational and irrational; the "rational" types are those whose dominant process is thinking or feeling, and the "irrational" are those whose dominant process is sensing or intuition. This distinction is of little practical use in ascertaining a person's type. The rationality of the introverted feeling type, for example, is too interior and subtle for the observer to perceive with any certainty, or even for the subject to report. It is safer to depend on relatively simple and accessible reactions.

The JP preference does show itself in simple and accessible reactions. It serves admirably as the fourth dichotomy if one detail is borne in mind: It deals only with outward behavior and thus points only indirectly to the dominant process of the introvert. The preference has three main advantages. It is easily ascertained; it is descriptive, embracing a number of conspicuous and important qualities; and it expresses a basic division in positive terms, without offense to either side. Both judging people and perceptive people can see merit in what they are, while to most people "irrational" is a fighting word.[3]

Inclusion of the JP preference in the theory came about as a result of unpublished personality research by Katharine C. Briggs before Jung's *Psychological Types* was published. The type categories she had devised were entirely consistent with Jung's, but less detailed. Her "meditative type" included all introvert types. Her "spontaneous type" corresponded to the perceptive extraverts, in whom perceptive behavior is at its strongest. Her "executive type" exactly described the extraverted thinkers, and her "sociable type" the extraverted feeling people.

When Jung's theory was published in 1923, she saw that it went far beyond her own, and she made an intensive study of it. Putting together the sentences quoted earlier in this chapter, she interpreted them to mean that the auxiliary process runs the introvert's outer life. She looked at the outer lives of her "meditative" friends to see if this was true and concluded that it was.

Briggs also found that when the introvert's auxiliary was a perceptive process, it gave rise to a perceptive attitude and an outer personality that resembled, in a quiet way, the "spontaneous" personality of the perceptive extravert. When the auxiliary was a judging process, it produced a judging attitude and an outer personality that was the opposite of "spontaneous."

Her own understanding of the "spontaneous" types had prepared her to recognize the perceptive attitude and the judging attitude—and the fact that they made a fourth pair of opposites. Inclusion of JP along with the other preferences, EI, SN, and TF, completed the system. The analyses she drew up at that time—summarizing the effects of each of these four preferences—provided, long afterward, the key to the practical determination of type.[4]

Reality of the Opposites

In all our subsequent work with type, Katharine Briggs and I have taken these four pairs of opposites as basic. We did not invent or discover them. They are inherent in Jung's theory of the function types, which is based on many years of observations that seemed to him to synthesize already existing knowledge of personality. We have been less interested in defining the processes than in describing the *consequences* of each preference as far as we can observe or infer them, and in using the most accessible consequences (not the most important) to develop a means of identifying type.

Since the more superficial aspects of type are often the easiest to report, many trivial reactions are useful for identification, but these are merely straws to show which way the wind blows. They are not the wind. It would be a mistake to assume that the essence of an attitude or of a perceptive or judging process is defined by its trivial surface effects or by the test items that reflect it or by the words used to describe it. The essence of each of the four preferences is an observable reality.

It is easy for people to see that they have a choice of two worlds on which to concentrate their interest. One is an outer world where things happen outside individuals or "without" them, in both senses of the word, and the other is an inner world where the activity is within the individual's mind, so that the individual is an inseparable part of all that goes on.

It will be apparent to people, too, though perhaps more clearly as applied to others rather than to themselves, that people have a choice of two attitudes in dealing with the outer world. They can perceive it with no inclination to judge it at the moment, or they can judge it without making any further effort at perception.

When people consider their own mental processes, it will be evident that more than one kind of perception is possible. People are certainly not limited to the direct report of their senses. Through the subtle messages of intuition people can also become aware of what might be or can be made to be.

Finally, people can see, at least in others, that there are two kinds of judgment, one by way of thinking and one by way of feeling. Everyone meets both daily, sometimes used appropriately and sometimes not.

The existence of the opposites is thus nothing new, as Jung himself points out. They are common knowledge, once people stop to think about them. The difficulty is, Jung notes, that they look quite different to different types. People of each type experience the opposites after their own fashion. Even with "perfect" knowledge of all sixteen points of view, it would still be impossible to define the opposites in terms that would satisfy everyone. However, when people waive formal definitions and consult instead the reality of their own experiences, they can agree that in each of the four areas just mentioned there is a choice of opposites that may be experienced, however the dichotomies are defined.

The new insight by which Jung synthesized such knowledge was the realization that an initial choice between these basic opposites *determines the line of development* for the person's perception and judgment and thus has profound consequences in the field of personality. This magnificent idea makes possible a coherent explanation for a variety of simple human differences, for complexities of personality, and for widely different satisfactions and motivations. It also suggests an important new dimension in understanding the development of young people.

Jung saw his theory as an aid to self-understanding, but the application of the theory (like the theory itself) extends beyond the point where Jung was content to stop. The type concepts shed light on the way individuals perceive and judge and on the things that they value most; the type concepts are thus useful whenever one person must communicate with another or live with another or make decisions that affect another's life.

PART II

Effects of the Preferences
on Personality

CHAPTER 3

Type Tables for Comparison and Discovery

SINCE PEOPLE OF each type must experience the opposites in their own way, readers will naturally see the type theory and the actual consequences of the preferences from their own points of view, in the light of the preferences which they themselves hold. The discussions in the following chapters, and the statistics that readers may gather, will mean much more to them after they have seen the types for themselves.

Therefore, people who work with the Type Indicator should observe the preferences in action and compare the descriptions with the everyday behavior of the types. Observers may notice new things and wish to amend the descriptions to fit their own opinions. The important thing is to gain a first-hand understanding of the types.

The obvious obstacle is that there are sixteen types, which are too many to keep in mind by brute memory. Their distinguishing qualities can best be seen by comparison and contrast. The easiest way to remember what is read and observed about each type is to populate a "Type Table" with family and friends.

The Type Table is a device for seeing all the types *in relation to each other*. It arranges the types so that those in specific areas of the Table have certain preferences in common and hence share whatever qualities arise from those preferences. It is therefore valuable both for analysis of research data and for systematic personal observation. Personalized with the names of friends and family, the Type Table and the type differences come to life.

It is a great convenience in using the Type Table to know where each type is without hunting for it. The following aids to memory will help.

Starting with perception, one of the earliest and most observable choices, the Type Table first divides for SN. All the sensing types go in the left half; all the intuitive types in the right half. It is easy to remember which half is which: in the expression "SN preference," S is on the left and N is on the right. So the first step is:

Sensing Types	IntuitiveTypes
–S—	–N—

Next comes judgment, possibly the next most discernible choice. Dividing each half for TF produces the four combinations of perception and judgment. The two columns with feeling are side by side in the middle, and the two columns with thinking have the outermost locations. This arrangement reflects the closer relationships feeling types have with other people, whereas thinking types are more detached. The second step, therefore, is:

Sensing Types		Intuitive Types	
Thinking	Feeling	Feeling	Thinking
–ST–	–SF–	–NF–	–NT–

Remember that in going from one combination to the next, only one preference changes at a time. Thus each combination has one process in common with those nearest to it.

The next step is to divide for EI. The introvert types go in the upper or "northern" half of the Type Table, where, in the best New England tradition, they can be thought of as silent, reserved, slow to unbend, and inclined to mind their own business and leave others to do the same. The extravert types, who can be thought of as being more open, accessible, communicative, and friendly, go in the lower or "southern" half. (No geographical differences in type should be inferred from this.) So the third step is:

	Sensing Types		Intuitive Types	
	Thinking	Feeling	Feeling	Thinking
Introvert	IST–	ISF–	INF–	INT–
Extravert	EST–	ESF–	ENF–	ENT–

The final division, for JP, divides each horizontal row into two, and the result is the complete Type Table with four rows and four columns,

Figure 2. The Type Table

		Sensing Types		Intuitive Types	
		Thinking −ST−	Feeling −SF−	Feeling −NF−	Thinking −NT−
Introvert	I − − J	ISTJ	ISFJ	INFJ	INTJ
	I − − P	ISTP	ISFP	INFP	INTP
Extravert	E − − P	ESTP	ESFP	ENFP	ENTP
	E − − J	ESTJ	ESFJ	ENFJ	ENTJ

as shown in Figure 2. The arrangement of the horizontal rows is designed to place at the bottom the E—Js, extraverts with the judging attitude. The E—Ps, the perceptive extraverts, come just above them. Next, *changing only one preference at a time*, come the I—P types, the perceptive introverts. The top row is occupied by the I—J types, the judging introverts, balancing the judging extraverts at the bottom. Thus, the more resistant types, the thinkers at left and right and the judging types at top and bottom, make a sort of wall around the Type Table; the "gentler" FP types are inside. The types with both of the resistant preferences, the tough-minded, executive TJs, occupy the four corners.

With these devices in mind—SN going from left to right, the feeling columns affiliating with each other in the center, the "northern" introverts and "southern" extraverts, and the judging types taking the brunt at the top and bottom—the Type Table can be remembered and reproduced from memory. More important, the Type Table makes a logical framework within which to store the characteristics of the types.

A full-size Type Table is printed at the end of this book (see pages 208 and 209). For each of the types, there is enough space for readers to list names and, if desired, occupations of friends, family, co-workers, and so on, who fit the different types. Once the Table is well-populated, the differences between extraverts and introverts can be clarified by contrasting the people in the lower half with those in the upper half. The SN preference will be illustrated by the contrast between the left and right halves, the TF preference by the contrast between the outermost and middle columns, and the JP preference by the way the people in the top and bottom rows differ from those in the middle rows.

With the effects of the separate preferences thus established, various areas of the Type Table take on a definite character from the *interaction* of these preferences. It seems natural that many psychiatrists are found in the intuition-plus-feeling column. It is clear why would-be young executives are often TJ. It is reasonable that students at the Wharton School of Finance and Commerce are most often ES and those at Cal Tech are most often IN.

Conversely, when a sample defined by occupation, college major, years of education, or any propensity are distributed in a Type Table, a concentration in an area of the Table may point out new facts about the *types in that area.*

For identifying types and groups of types, letters are more precise and convenient than words. A group of types with one or more preferences in common can be defined precisely by the common letter(s), arranged in standard order, with dashes where the letters are not adjacent.

In this book, a type designation is to be taken in its broadest sense. The eight types in the left half of the Type Table are therefore all *sensing types*, and the eight types in the right half are all *intuitives*.

On the other hand, the qualified term *introverted intuitive* always means an introvert in whom intuition is dominant, an IN–J type; the term *extraverted intuitive* always means an extravert in whom intuition dominates, an EN–P. Similarly, *introverted sensing* type refers to an IS–J and *extraverted sensing* type means an ES–P, and so on. These are the formal names of Jung's original eight types.

The preposition *with*, as used throughout this book, denotes the combination of two preferences without reference to dominance. The four IN types in the upper right quarter of the Type Table are "introverts with intuition"; the types in the NF column are "intuitives with feeling"; and so on.

The Type Tables in Figures 3–23 show the meanings of the letter combinations and, more important, illustrate the use of frequencies in making discoveries about the individual types. If a particular type is much more (or much less) frequent in a given sample than expected, the characteristics of the type may be responsible for this distribution.

In exploring such hypotheses, it is necessary to adopt a reasonable estimate of the frequency to be expected for those types. Most of the Type Tables in this chapter adopt for this purpose the frequencies actually found in a sample of 3,503 high school males preparing for college, as

Figure 3. High School Students, College Prep
(*N* = 3,503 males)

Sensing Types with Thinking	Sensing Types with Feeling	Intuitive Types with Feeling	Intuitive Types with Thinking	
ISTJ N=283 8.1% ■■■■	ISFJ N=139 4.0% ■■	INFJ N=74 2.1% ■	INTJ N=164 4.7% ■	Introverts Judging Perceptive
ISTP N=180 5.1% ■■	ISFP N=153 4.4% ■	INFP N=146 4.2% ■	INTP N=209 6.0% ■■	
ESTP N=271 7.7% ■■	ESFP N=225 6.4% ■■	ENFP N=250 7.1% ■■	ENTP N=276 7.9% ■■	Extraverts Perceptive Judging
ESTJ N=549 15.7% ■■■■	ESFJ N=227 6.5% ■■	ENFJ N=124 3.5% ■	ENTJ N=233 6.6% ■■	

	N	%	N	%	
E	2,155	61.5	2,165	61.8	T
I	1,348	38.5	1,338	38.2	F
S	2,027	57.9	1,793	51.2	J
N	1,476	42.1	1,710	48.8	P

shown in the Type Table in Figure 3. The samples in Figures 5 and 8 were combined to make this group, which was also used for the expected frequencies on page 45 of the 1962 *Myers-Briggs Type Indicator Manual*.

The Type Tables in Figures 3–23 show the heaviest frequencies and the areas with relatively sparse populations. In these Figures, the percent of the sample belonging to each type is written *and* shown graphically either with black squares, each representing roughly 2 percent, or with black circles, each standing for approximately 2 persons. (Circles are used in Figures 16, 17, 18, and 20, in which the samples are less than 100.) The total number of extraverts, introverts, and so on and the percentage each number represents are given below the Tables.

Figure 4. High School Students, Other Than College Prep
(N = 1,430 males)

ISTJ N=149 10.4%	ISFJ N=82 5.7%	INFJ N=5 0.3%	INTJ N=18 1.3%
ISTP N=122 8.5%	ISFP N=102 7.1%	INFP N=26 1.8%	INTP N=27 1.9%
ESTP N=168 11.8%	ESFP N=129 9.0%	ENFP N=45 3.2%	ENTP N=40 2.8%
ESTJ N=293 20.5%	ESFJ N=178 12.5%	ENFJ N=16 1.1%	ENTJ N=30 2.1%

	N	%	N	%	
E	899	62.9	847	59.2	T
I	531	37.1	583	40.8	F
S	1,223	85.5	771	53.9	J
N	207	14.5	659	46.1	P

The Type Tables in Figures 4 and 5 show male high school students, mainly eleventh- and twelfth-graders, who took Form D2 of the Indicator in 25 high schools in the suburban counties around Philadelphia in the spring of 1957, a period when sharp distinctions were maintained between college preparatory and nonpreparatory high school programs.[5] The greatest contrast here is between the low incidence of intuitives among the nonprep students compared with the substantial 38 percent of intuitives among the college preparatory students.

Figure 5. High School Students, College Prep
(*N* = 2,603 males)

ISTJ N=216 8.3%	ISFJ N=105 4.0%	INFJ N=52 2.0%	INTJ N=108 4.1%
ISTP N=151 5.8%	ISFP N=126 4.8%	INFP N=103 4.0%	INTP N=145 5.6%
ESTP N=218 8.4%	ESFP N=193 7.4%	ENFP N=170 6.5%	ENTP N=184 7.1%
ESTJ N=440 16.9%	ESFJ N=164 6.3%	ENFJ N=78 3.0%	ENTJ N=150 5.8%

	N	%		N	%	
E	1,597	61.4		1,612	61.9	T
I	1,006	38.6		991	38.1	F
S	1,613	62.0		1,313	50.4	J
N	990	38.0		1,290	49.6	P

On preferences other than SN, the differences in frequency are minimal. In both Tables the most frequent type is an S type, ESTJ, and the least frequent is an N type, INFJ. Otherwise these samples reveal fairly equal distributions, which is appropriate enough, since high school students are a heterogeneous group of very different people who will eventually ride off in all directions. College Type Tables (Figures 12–19) show some of those directions.

Figure 6. High School Students, Other Than College Prep
(N = 1,884 females)

ISTJ N=120 6.4%	ISFJ N=240 12.7%	INFJ N=13 0.7%	INTJ N=7 0.4%
ISTP N=36 1.9%	ISFP N=125 6.6%	INFP N=36 1.9%	INTP N=14 0.7%
ESTP N=84 4.5%	ESFP N=259 13.7%	ENFP N=95 5.0%	ENTP N=15 0.8%
ESTJ N=305 16.2%	ESFJ N=476 25.3%	ENFJ N=46 2.5%	ENTJ N=13 0.7%

	N	%	N	%	
E	1,293	68.6	594	31.5	T
I	591	31.4	1,290	68.5	F
S	1,645	87.3	1,220	64.8	J
N	239	12.7	664	35.2	P

The corresponding Type Tables for females, Figures 6 and 7, confirm the relation between intuition and educational level; they also demonstrate the magnitude of the sex difference on TF. Both female samples are 68 percent feeling; the nonpreparatory males are 41 percent feeling, the college preparatory males 38 percent. Because of this sex difference, data involving type frequencies for males and females must be presented separately; if pooled, the frequencies misrepresent both sexes.

Figure 7. High School Students, College Prep
(N = 2,155 females)

ISTJ N=72 3.3%	ISFJ N=149 6.9%	INFJ N=59 2.7%	INTJ N=39 1.8%
ISTP N=47 2.2%	ISFP N=105 4.9%	INFP N=136 6.3%	INTP N=66 3.1%
ESTP N=75 3.5%	ESFP N=243 11.3%	ENFP N=269 12.5%	ENTP N=111 5.2%
ESTJ N=210 9.7%	ESFJ N=380 17.6%	ENFJ N=123 5.7%	ENTJ N=71 3.3%

	N	%	N	%	
E	1,482	68.8	691	32.1	T
I	673	31.2	1,464	67.9	F
S	1,281	59.4	1,103	51.2	J
N	874	40.6	1,052	48.8	P

The sensing types in Figures 6 and 7 show a strong preference for the judging attitude. The nonpreparatory sample, which has very few intuitives, is 65 percent J. Sensing types prefer, on the whole, to run their outer lives in a judging way that settles problems in advance. Intuitives like to run theirs in a perceptive way that lets their intuition follow its inspirations.

Figure 8. Central High School Students
(N = 900 males)

ISTJ N=67 7.4%	ISFJ N=34 3.8%	INFJ N=22 2.5%	INTJ N=56 6.2%
ISTP N=29 3.2%	ISFP N=27 3.0%	INFP N=43 4.8%	INTP N=64 7.1%
ESTP N=53 5.9%	ESFP N=32 3.6%	ENFP N=80 8.9%	ENTP N=92 10.2%
ESTJ N=109 12.1%	ESFJ N=63 7.0%	ENFJ N=46 5.1%	ENTJ N=83 9.2%

	N	%	N	%	
E	558	62.0	553	61.4	T
I	342	38.0	347	38.6	F
S	414	46.0	480	53.3	J
N	486	54.0	420	46.7	P

The Type Table in Figure 8 shows high school males preparing for college—but these students were preparing at the all-male Central High School in Philadelphia, to which no student is admitted unless he has an IQ of 110 or higher and no more than one grade as low as C in the two years before enrolling.

It might be thought that the second requirement, which involves not seriously slighting any subject, would result in a substantial increase in the number of J students. The number of J students did go up, but only from 50.4 percent to 53.3 percent.

Figure 9. National Merit Finalists
(N = 671 males)

ISTJ N=36 5.4%	ISFJ N=7 1.0%	INFJ N=31 4.6%	INTJ N=110 16.4%
ISTP N=21 3.1%	ISFP N=6 0.9%	INFP N=81 12.1%	INTP N=107 15.9%
ESTP N=7 1.0%	ESFP N=10 1.5%	ENFP N=62 9.2%	ENTP N=78 11.6%
ESTJ N=23 3.5%	ESFJ N=6 0.9%	ENFJ N=28 4.2%	ENTJ N=58 8.7%

	N	%	N	%	
E	272	40.5	440	65.6	T
I	399	59.5	231	34.4	F
S	116	17.3	299	44.6	J
N	555	82.7	372	55.4	P

The frequency of N went up from 38 percent to 54 percent, which resulted in a symmetrical lowering of the frequencies of the four SP types, who have neither N nor J.

For the National Merit finalists, Figure 9, the frequency of N went up from 54 percent to 82.7 percent. Of the remaining 17.3 percent who were S, the outstanding survivor was ISTJ, holding 5 percent of the sample.

Figure 10. Philadelphia Girls' High School Students
(N = 348 females)

ISTJ N=21 6.0%	ISFJ N=26 7.5%	INFJ N=16 4.6%	INTJ N=16 4.6%
ISTP N=3 0.9%	ISFP N=18 5.2%	INFP N=19 5.4%	INTP N=14 4.0%
ESTP N=10 2.9%	ESFP N=17 4.9%	ENFP N=49 14.1%	ENTP N=14 4.0%
ESTJ N=38 10.9%	ESFJ N=41 11.8%	ENFJ N=27 7.8%	ENTJ N=19 5.4%

	N	%	N	%	
E	215	61.8	135	38.8	T
I	133	38.2	213	61.2	F
S	174	50.0	204	58.6	J
N	174	50.0	144	41.4	P

The corresponding selective high school for females is Philadelphia Girls' High School, which has the same requirements for admission as Central. Frequency distributions in the Type Tables in Figures 10 and 11 are much like those for the corresponding male samples, except that the males have a majority for T, whereas the females have a majority for F, as has been seen before.

Introverts at Girls' High are 38.2 percent, rising to 52.1 percent among the National Merit finalists.

Intuitives at Girls' High are 50 percent, rising to 81.8 percent in the National Merit sample.

Figure 11. National Merit Finalists
(*N* = 330 females)

ISTJ N=10 3.0% ∎∎	ISFJ N=17 5.2% ∎∎	INFJ ∎ N=36 ∎ 10.9% ∎∎	INTJ ∎ N=29 ∎ 8.8% ∎
ISTP N=4 1.2% ∎	ISFP N=5 1.5% ∎	INFP ∎ N=38 ∎ 11.5% ∎∎	INTP ∎ N=33 ∎ 10.0% ∎∎
ESTP N=0 0%	ESFP N=10 3.0% ∎	ENFP ∎∎ N=61 ∎∎ 18.5% ∎∎∎	ENTP ∎ N=32 ∎ 9.7% ∎∎
ESTJ N=7 2.1% ∎	ESFJ N=7 2.1% ∎	ENFJ ∎ N=26 ∎ 7.9% ∎	ENTJ N=15 4.6% ∎

	N	%	N	%	
E	158	47.9	130	39.4	T
I	172	52.1	200	60.6	F
S	60	18.2	147	44.5	J
N	270	81.8	183	55.5	P

As with ISTJ for the males, the outstanding survivor of the S types among the female National Merit finalists was ISFJ, with a 5 percent frequency matching that of the males.

Here self-selection begins. After high school, students can choose whatever line of study they like. The degree of self-selection exercised by any type in any sample can be indicated by the *self-selection ratio* (SSR), which is the percentage frequency of that type in the sample divided by its percentage frequency in the appropriate base population. For the samples in this chapter, except for the arts and counseling students, the base population is 3,503 high school males (Figure 3).

Gifts Differing

Figure 12. Liberal Arts Students
(*N* = 3,676 males)

ISTJ ∎	ISFJ	INFJ	INTJ ∎
N=269	N=154	N=185	N=267
7.3%	4.2%	5.0%	7.3%
SSR=0.91	SSR=1.06	SSR=2.38	SSR=1.55
ISTP	ISFP	INFP	INTP
N=120	N=103	N=294	N=287
3.3%	2.8%	8.0%	7.8%
SSR=0.64	SSR=0.64	SSR=1.92	SSR=1.31
ESTP	ESFP	ENFP	ENTP
N=138	N=157	N=353	N=298
3.8%	4.3%	9.6%	8.1%
SSR=0.49	SSR=0.66	SSR=1.35	SSR=1.03
ESTJ	ESFJ	ENFJ	ENTJ
N=343	N=218	N=214	N=276
9.3%	5.9%	5.8%	7.5%
SSR=0.60	SSR=0.92	SSR=1.64	SSR=1.13

	N	%	N	%	
E	1,997	54.3	1,998	54.4	T
I	1,679	45.7	1,678	45.6	F
S	1,502	40.9	1,926	52.4	J
N	2,174	59.1	1,750	47.6	P

In Figures 12–23, the SSR is shown for each of the sixteen types. Values above 1.00 show positive self-selection. Values below 1.00 show some degree of avoidance. Where types with the highest SSR (often 1.20 or higher) are adjacent, they make a self-selection area and are shaded in the Type Table.

For the males in liberal arts, shown in Figure 12, the self-selection area consists of the four NF types, typically interested in literature and humanities, and the two INT types, mildly interested in liberal arts but more interested in other fields.

Figure 13. Engineering Students
(*N* = 2,188)

ISTJ N=222 10.1% SSR=1.26	ISFJ N=92 4.2% SSR=1.06	INFJ N=115 5.3% SSR=2.49	INTJ N=301 13.8% SSR=2.94
ISTP N=49 2.2% SSR=0.44	ISFP N=42 1.9% SSR=0.44	INFP N=110 5.0% SSR=1.21	INTP N=191 8.7% SSR=1.46
ESTP N=67 3.1% SSR=0.40	ESFP N=29 1.3% SSR=0.21	ENFP N=124 5.7% SSR=0.79	ENTP N=159 7.3% SSR=0.92
ESTJ N=197 9.0% SSR=0.57	ESFJ N=72 3.3% SSR=0.51	ENFJ N=134 6.1% SSR=1.73	ENTJ N=284 13.0% SSR=1.95

	N	%	N	%	
E	1,066	48.7	1,470	67.2	T
I	1,122	51.3	718	32.8	F
S	770	35.2	1,417	64.8	J
N	1,418	64.8	771	35.2	P

For the engineering students, shown in Figure 13, the self-selection area consists of the IN quadrant, the two ENJ types, and ISTJ. The emphasis is on N and J, and F when combined with NJ seems nearly as attracted to engineering as T. Note that the ENJ types would be adjacent to the IN quadrant if wrapped around a horizontal cylinder, and so would ISTJ if wrapped around a vertical one.

(These are the liberal arts and engineering samples from page 45 of the 1962 MBTI Manual.)

Figure 14. Finance and Commerce Students
(*N* = 488)

ISTJ N=44 9.0% SSR=1.12	ISFJ N=19 3.9% SSR=0.98	INFJ N=1 0.2% SSR=0.10	INTJ N=13 2.7% SSR=0.57
ISTP N=35 7.2% SSR=1.40	ISFP N=7 1.4% SSR=0.33	INFP N=11 2.3% SSR=0.54	INTP N=15 3.1% SSR=0.52
ESTP N=63 12.9% SSR=1.67	ESFP N=34 7.0% SSR=1.08	ENFP N=30 6.1% SSR=0.86	ENTP N=35 7.2% SSR=0.91
ESTJ N=106 21.7% SSR=1.39	ESFJ N=43 8.8% SSR=1.36	ENFJ N=8 1.6% SSR=0.46	ENTJ N=24 4.9% SSR=0.74

	N	%	N	%	
E	343	70.3	335	68.6	T
I	145	29.7	153	31.4	F
S	351	71.9	258	52.9	J
N	137	28.1	230	47.1	P

The Type Table in Figure 14 shows 488 undergraduates from the Wharton School of Finance and Commerce at the University of Pennsylvania. The Type Table opposite, in Figure 15, is really opposite, showing 705 science majors from Cal Tech.

The self-selection area for the finance and commerce students consists of the ES quadrant plus the two IST types, which is wholly suitable. The ST column is the one where the main objects of interest are the facts, approached with impersonal analysis, in a hardheaded, matter-of-fact way. The ES quadrant is the most practical and realistic quadrant and the least given to intellectual abstractions.

Figure 15. Science Students
(N = 705)

ISTJ	ISFJ	INFJ	INTJ
N=39	N=12	N=44	N=128
5.5%	1.7%	6.3%	18.2%
SSR=0.68	SSR=0.43	SSR=2.95	SSR=3.88
ISTP	ISFP	INFP	INTP
N=18	N=15	N=58	N=123
2.6%	2.1%	8.2%	17.5%
SSR=0.50	SSR=0.49	SSR=1.97	SSR=2.92
ESTP	ESFP	ENFP	ENTP
N=12	N=1	N=55	N=79
1.7%	0.1%	7.8%	11.2%
SSR=0.22	SSR=0.02	SSR=1.09	SSR=1.42
ESTJ	ESFJ	ENFJ	ENTJ
N=13	N=8	N=27	N=73
1.8%	1.1%	3.8%	10.4%
SSR=0.12	SSR=0.18	SSR=1.08	SSR=1.56

	N	%	N	%	
E	268	38.0	485	68.8	T
I	437	62.0	220	31.2	F
S	118	16.7	344	48.8	J
N	587	83.3	361	51.2	P

The self-selection area for the Cal Tech science students consists of the IN quadrant (in which the highest SSR is 3.88 and the lowest one 1.97) plus the two ENT types. People in the NT column focus on the possibilities and the principles involved in their solution. Inhabitants of the IN quadrant are the most intellectual, with a capacity for seeing farther into the unknown than most people can penetrate. The degree of interest that the science students have for the ES quadrant can be judged by the self-selection ratios they award it: 0.22, 0.17, 0.12, and 0.02.

Figure 16. Fine Arts Seniors
(*N* = 33)

ISTJ N=0 0% SSR=0.0	ISFJ N=0 0% SSR=0.0	INFJ N=3 9.1% SSR=2.02	INTJ N=4 12.1% SSR=2.96
ISTP N=1 3.0% SSR=0.95	ISFP N=1 3.0% SSR=0.57	INFP N=10 30.4% SSR=2.73	INTP N=6 18.3% SSR=3.60
ESTP N=0 0% SSR=0.0	ESFP N=0 0% SSR=0.0	ENFP N=4 12.1% SSR=0.86	ENTP N=0 0% SSR=0.0
ESTJ N=0 0% SSR=0.0	ESFJ N=1 3.0% SSR=0.36	ENFJ N=1 3.0% SSR=0.46	ENTJ N=2 6.0% SSR=1.40

	N	%	N	%	
E	8	24.2	13	39.4	T
I	25	75.8	20	60.6	F
S	3	9.1	11	33.3	J
N	30	90.9	22	66.7	P

Source: Stephens (1972)

The Type Tables in Figures 16–18, based on Stephens (1972), present three contrasting groups of senior art students at the University of Florida. The base population against which their self-selection is measured is a freshman class at the same university at about the same period.

The sample in Figure 16 consists of fine arts seniors who were planning to *be* artists, to create without reference to others. The four types showing positive self-selection are all IN types—intuition for creativity and introversion for independence from the outer world.

Figure 17. Occupational Therapy Seniors
(N = 29)

ISTJ N=0 0% SSR=0.0	ISFJ N=2 6.9% ● SSR=1.03	INFJ N=1 3.4% ● SSR=0.77	INTJ N=1 3.4% ● SSR=0.84
ISTP N=0 0% SSR=0.0	ISFP N=0 0% SSR=0.0	INFP N=2 6.9% ● SSR=0.62	INTP N=1 3.4% ● SSR=0.68
ESTP N=0 0% SSR=0.0	ESFP N=2 6.9% ● SSR=1.20	ENFP ● N=9 ● 31.1% ●● SSR=2.21	ENTP N=3 10.4% ● SSR=2.11
ESTJ N=0 0% SSR=0.0	ESFJ ● N=6 ● 20.7% ● SSR=2.48	ENFJ N=2 6.9% ● SSR=1.05	ENTJ N=0 0% SSR=0.0

	N	%		N	%	
E	22	75.9		5	17.2	T
I	7	24.1		24	82.8	F
S	10	34.5		12	41.4	J
N	19	65.5		17	58.6	P

Source: Stephens (1972)

The seniors in Figure 17 were studying occupational therapy and planning to use art for restoring people to health, whether by giving them a new interest in life or new confidence in themselves or simply an enjoyable manual activity. All five of the types showing positive self-selection are extravert types, to whom overt action is important, and four of those five types are F types, to whom it is important that the action involve other people in a beneficial way. The type with the strongest self-selection is ESFJ, where feeling is extraverted and perception is practical, so that helping others is both a duty and a pleasure.

Figure 18. Art Education Seniors
(*N* = 31)

ISTJ N=0 0% SSR=0.00	ISFJ N=0 0% SSR=0.00	INFJ N=3 9.7% SSR=2.15	INTJ N=1 3.2% SSR=0.79
ISTP N=0 0% SSR=0.00	ISFP N=0 0% SSR=0.00	INFP N=8 25.8% SSR=2.33	INTP N=4 12.9% SSR=2.55
ESTP N=0 0% SSR=0.00	ESFP N=1 3.2% SSR=0.56	ENFP N=7 22.5% SSR=1.61	ENTP N=2 6.5% SSR=1.32
ESTJ N=0 0% SSR=0.00	ESFJ N=3 9.7% SSR=1.16	ENFJ N=2 6.5% SSR=0.98	ENTJ N=0 0% SSR=0.00

	N	%	N	%	
E	15	48.4	7	22.6	T
I	16	51.6	24	77.4	F
S	4	12.9	9	29.0	J
N	27	87.1	22	71.0	P

Source: Stephens (1972)

In examining Figure 18, which reports on art education seniors, one finds a wide diversity of types who have chosen that field, perhaps because the field itself is diverse. This sample has six types with positive self-selection, three in common with fine arts students, three in common with occupational therapy students; three are I, three are E; three are NF, two are NT, and one is the somewhat detached SF. Probably the teaching styles these people developed would be found to vary accordingly.

Figure 19. Counselor Education Students
(*N* = 118)

ISTJ N=4 3.4% SSR=0.53	ISFJ N=2 1.7% SSR=0.25	INFJ N=11 9.3% SSR=2.07	INTJ N=3 2.5% SSR=0.62
ISTP N=1 0.8% SSR=0.27	ISFP N=2 1.7% SSR=0.32	INFP N=28 23.8% SSR=2.14	INTP N=3 2.5% SSR=0.50
ESTP N=0 0% SSR=0.0	ESFP N=3 2.5% SSR=0.44	ENFP N=37 31.4% SSR=2.23	ENTP N=2 1.7% SSR=0.35
ESTJ N=2 1.7% SSR=0.22	ESFJ N=4 3.4% SSR=0.41	ENFJ N=14 11.9% SSR=1.81	ENTJ N=2 1.7% SSR=0.39

	N	%	N	%	
E	64	54.2	17	14.4	T
I	54	45.8	101	85.6	F
S	18	15.2	42	35.6	J
N	100	84.8	76	64.4	P

In Figure 19, counselor education, self-selection seems confined to the NF types. Each NF type has a self-selection ratio of 1.80 or higher, and no other type has a self-selection ratio higher than 0.62. The reason is easily understood: The combination of intuition and feeling practically defines counseling. The province of intuition is to see the possibilities, and the province of feeling is a concern for people, which makes the exercise of intuition doubly rewarding, since it is possibilities *for people* that are sought and found.

The subjects in this sample were students at the University of Florida who gave their major as counseling education. For their SSRs also, the base population was the Florida freshmen.

Figure 20. Rhodes Scholars
(*N* = 71 males)

ISTJ N=0 0% SSR=0.0	ISFJ N=1 1.4% ● SSR=0.35	INFJ N=5 ●● 7.0% ● SSR=3.33	INTJ ● N=8 ●● 11.3% ● SSR=2.41
ISTP N=1 1.4% ● SSR=0.27	ISFP N=1 1.4% ● SSR=0.32	INFP ●● N=15 ●● 21.1% ●● SSR=5.07	INTP ● N=10 ●● 14.1% ●● SSR=2.36
ESTP N=0 0% SSR=0.0	ESFP N=1 1.4% ● SSR=0.22	ENFP ● N=9 ●● 12.7% ●● SSR=1.78	ENTP ● N=8 ●● 11.3% ● SSR=1.43
ESTJ N=0 0% SSR=0.0	ESFJ N=1 1.4% ● SSR=0.22	ENFJ ● N=6 ●● 8.5% ● SSR=2.39	ENTJ ● N=5 ●● 7.0% ● SSR=1.06

	N	%	N	%	
E	30	42.3	32	45.1	T
I	41	57.7	39	54.9	F
S	5	7.0	26	36.6	J
N	66	93.0	45	63.4	P

The sample of Rhodes Scholars, shown in Figure 20, is the result of stringent competition. It has an even higher percentage of intuitives than the National Merit finalists. The majority are feeling types, probably because in defining the scholar Rhodes desired, his will stressed kindness and interest in others.

Figure 21 is based on data from Miller's follow-up study (1967) of students from seven law schools, including the dropouts. The number of dropouts from each type is shown, preceded by a minus sign, on the same line as the frequency for that type. The dropout ratio (DOR), which is the type's percentage dropout divided by the percentage dropout for the sample as a whole, is given below the SSR.

Figure 21. Law Students
(*N* = 2,248—374 of whom dropped out)

ISTJ	ISFJ	INFJ	INTJ
N=236 −28	N=58 −13	N=58 −8	N=194 −22
10.5%	2.6%	2.6%	8.6%
SSR=1.43	SSR=0.62	SSR=0.51	SSR=1.19
DOR=0.71	DOR=1.34	DOR=0.82	DOR=0.68
ISTP	ISFP	INFP	INTP
N=87 −18	N=33 −7	N=120 −31	N=221 −42
3.9%	1.5%	5.3%	9.8%
SSR=1.19	SSR=0.52	SSR=0.67	SSR=1.26
DOR=1.23	DOR=1.25	DOR=1.56	DOR=1.15
ESTP	ESFP	ENFP	ENTP
N=87 −12	N=42 −6	N=132 −32	N=245 −46
3.9%	1.9%	5.9%	10.9%
SSR=1.03	SSR=0.44	SSR=0.61	SSR=1.34
DOR=0.82	DOR=0.84	DOR=1.45	DOR=1.13
ESTJ	ESFJ	ENFJ	ENTJ
N=295 −44	N=80 −14	N=75 −14	N=285 −37
13.1%	3.5%	3.3%	12.7%
SSR=1.41	SSR=0.60	SSR=0.57	SSR=1.69
DOR=0.90	DOR=1.04	DOR=1.13	DOR=0.78

	N	%	N	%	
E	1,241	55.2	1,650	73.4	T
I	1,007	44.8	598	26.6	F
S	918	40.8	1,281	57.0	J
N	1,330	59.2	967	43.0	P

Source: Miller (1965,1967)

The results are very clear-cut. The essential for law is T, preferably TJ. All four of the TJ types have positive self-selection and a lower-than-average dropout rate. Three of the TP types have positive self-selection but a *higher-than-average* dropout rate. None of the feeling types have SSR above 0.67, and six of them have a higher-than-average dropout rate. Apparently law school is best tackled by the tough-minded.

Figure 22. Urban Police
(*N* = 280)

ISTJ N=39 13.9% SSR=1.72	ISFJ N=24 8.6% SSR=2.16	INFJ N=3 1.1% SSR=0.51	INTJ N=9 3.2% SSR=0.69
ISTP N=19 6.8% SSR=1.32	ISFP N=10 3.6% SSR=0.82	INFP N=6 2.1% SSR=0.51	INTP N=5 1.8% SSR=0.30
ESTP N=22 7.9% SSR=1.02	ESFP N=16 5.7% SSR=0.89	ENFP N=7 2.5% SSR=0.35	ENTP N=9 3.2% SSR=0.41
ESTJ N=72 25.7% SSR=1.64	ESFJ N=21 7.5% SSR=1.16	ENFJ N=6 2.1% SSR=0.61	ENTJ N=12 4.3% SSR=0.64

	N	%	N	%	
E	165	58.9	187	66.8	T
I	115	41.1	93	33.2	F
S	223	79.6	186	66.4	J
N	57	20.4	94	32.6	P

The sample of urban police, Figure 22, affords an interesting comparison with the law students just seen, because both groups deal with the law. The students deal with the subtle distinctions of the law, what one can and cannot do. They also face the endless prospect of dealing in words with adversaries also armed with words. These are good reasons why 59 percent of them are on the intuitive side.

The police are 79 percent S. They deal with one concrete situation after another, where words are not as important as decisions and actions. They are more J than the law students, and a good many more of them are feeling types. There may well be more compassion on the beat than in the courts of law.

Figure 23. School Administrators
(*N* = 124)

ISTJ ■ N=14 ■■ 11.3% ■■ SSR=1.40	ISFJ ■ N=12 ■ 9.7% ■■ SSR=2.44	INFJ ■ N=9 ■ 7.3% ■ SSR=3.44	INTJ ■ N=10 ■ 8.1% ■ SSR=1.72
ISTP N=0 0% SSR=0.0	ISFP N=1 0.8% SSR=0.18	INFP N=3 2.4% ■ SSR=0.58	INTP N=1 0.8% SSR=0.14
ESTP N=1 0.8% SSR=0.10	ESFP N=3 2.4% ■ SSR=0.38	ENFP N=6 4.8% ■ SSR=0.68	ENTP N=2 1.6% ■ SSR=0.20
ESTJ ■■ N=27 ■■■ 21.8% ■■■ SSR=1.39	ESFJ ■ N=15 ■■ 12.1% ■■ SSR=1.87	ENFJ ■ N=7 ■ 5.6% ■ SSR=1.59	ENTJ ■ N=13 ■ 10.5% ■■ SSR=1.58

	N	%		N	%	
E	74	59.7		68	54.8	T
I	50	40.3		56	45.2	F
S	73	58.9		107	86.3	J
N	51	41.1		17	13.7	P

Source: von Fange (1961)

The Type Table in Figure 23, which portrays von Fange's Canadian school administrators (1961), is unique. It is all top and bottom. The sample seems to have no marked preference between E and I, S and N, or T and F. However, in dealing with the world around them, they are 86 percent J. Probably the ability to make endless decisions, great and small, and not grow weary is a necessity of life for those responsible for keeping educational systems on an even keel.

CHAPTER 4

Effect of the EI Preference

THE CONDUCT OF extraverts is based on the outer situation. If they are thinkers, they tend to criticize or analyze or organize it; feeling types may champion it, protest against it, or try to mitigate it; sensing types may enjoy it, use it, or good naturedly put up with it; and intuitives tend to try to change it. In any case, the extravert starts with the outer situation.

The introvert, however, *starts* farther back—with the inner ideas, the mental concepts, derived from what Jung calls the archetypes. Type theory holds that the archetypes are inborn in us all. They do not have their origin in our own experience, though personal experience may activate them. They are the abstract essence of the experience and aspiration of humanity. They are the universals, the shapes of thought, which bring pattern and meaning out of the overwhelming multiplicity of life. (Extraverts find multiplicity rather jolly; but it can be intolerably distracting to introverts unless they can see a unifying meaning that brings it under control.)

When an outer situation encountered by introverts corresponds to a familiar idea or concept, they meet the situation with a sense of recognition, as though seeing a good illustration of something long known. For such situations the introverts have a profound understanding. If, however, the outer situation does not correspond at all to familiar concepts, it may seem accidental, irrelevant, and unimportant, and the introverts are very likely to mishandle it. One historic example is Woodrow Wilson's blindness at Versailles, when he staked the peace upon the League of Nations, a decision that his own country was not ready to accept. He was too wrapped up in the idea of world organization to give the idea of democratic process its due—so the Senate seemed irrelevant to him, and he failed.

Because introverts' energies are powerfully directed by their ideas, it is supremely important for introverts to have the "right idea" about things. Their characteristic pause before action, which extraverts carelessly call hesitation, serves a real purpose. It gives time to study and classify a new situation so the action taken will make sense in the long run. Problems arise for the introverts because they often do not look closely enough at the outer situation and, therefore, do not really see it. The extraverts often do not *stop* looking at the specific situation long enough to see the underlying idea.

The advantages of starting with the outer situation are obvious and much esteemed in the present Western civilization, which is dominated by the extravert viewpoint. There are plenty of reasons for this domination: Extraverts are more vocal than introverts; they are more numerous, apparently in the ratio of three to one;[6] and they are accessible and understandable, whereas the introverts are not readily understandable, even to each other, and are likely to be thoroughly incomprehensible to the extraverts.

Consequently, the introverts' advantages need to be pointed out— not only to the extraverts but sometimes even to the introverts themselves—for the best-adjusted people are the "psychologically patriotic," who are glad to be what they are. The ablest introverts achieve a fine facility at extraversion, but never try to *be* extraverts. Through good development of an auxiliary process, they have learned to deal competently with the outer world without pledging any allegiance to it. Their loyalty goes to their own inner principle and derives from it a secure and unshakable orientation to life.

One advantage of the introverts is their inherent continuity, an independence of the momentary outward situation, which often is as accidental as it seems to them. Outer conditions and stimuli continually vary, but inner stimuli are far more constant. Introvert children, entirely ignoring many of the distracting outer stimuli, follow their own quiet bent, and parents of restless little extraverts marvel at the introverts' "powers of concentration."

This faculty of concentration is likely to characterize the introverts' careers. Whereas extraverts tend to broaden the sphere of their work, to present their products early (and often) to the world, to make themselves known to a wide circle, and to multiply relationships and activities, the introvert takes the opposite approach. Going more deeply into their work, introverts are reluctant to call it finished and publish it, and when they do, they tend to give only their conclusions, without the details of what they did. This impersonal brevity of communication narrows their audience and fame, but saves them from overwhelming external demands and allows them to return to another uninterrupted stretch of work. As Jung is reported to have said, the introverts' activity thereby gains in depth and their labor has lasting value.

Another useful aspect of the detachment characteristic of introverts is that they are little affected by the absence of encouragement. If they believe in what they are doing, they can work happily for a long time without reassurance, as pioneers usually must. Such behavior does not make sense to most extraverts. One brilliant and very extraverted young woman (an ENTP) protested, "But I'm never sure whether my work is good or not until I know what other people think of it!"

Finally, although extraverts certainly have more worldly wisdom and a better sense of expediency, introverts have a corresponding advantage in unworldly wisdom. They are closer to the eternal truths. The contrast is especially apparent when an extravert and an introvert are brought up side by side in the same family. The introvert child is often able to grasp and accept a moral principle—"yours and mine," for example—in its abstract form. The extravert child is usually unimpressed by the abstract principle, and usually must experience it; then, having learned the hard way what others think, the extravert has a basis for conduct.

The contrasting traits resulting from the EI preference are summarized here in parallel columns in Figure 24. In general, these differences distinguish people in the lower half of the Type Table from those in the upper half.

Figure 24. Effect of the EI Preference

Extraverts	Introverts
The afterthinkers. Cannot understand life until they have lived it.	The forethinkers. Cannot live life until they understand it.
Attitude relaxed and confident. They expect the waters to prove shallow, and plunge readily into new and untried experiences.	Attitude reserved and questioning. They expect the waters to prove deep, and pause to take soundings in the new and untried.
Minds outwardly directed, interest and attention following objective happenings, primarily those of the immediate environment. Their real world therefore is the outer world of people and things.	Minds inwardly directed, frequently unaware of the objective environment, interest and attention being engrossed by inner events.Their real world therefore is the inner world of ideas and understanding.
The civilizing genius, the people of action and practical achievement, who go from doing to considering back to doing.	The cultural genius, the people of ideas and abstract invention, who go from considering to doing and back to considering.
Conduct in essential matters is always governed by objective conditions.	Conduct in essential matters is always governed by subjective values.
Spend themselves lavishly upon external claims and conditions which to them constitute life.	Defend themselves as far as possible against external claims and conditions in favor of the inner life.
Understandable and accessible, often sociable, more at home in the world of people and things than in the world of ideas.	Subtle and impenetrable, often taciturn and shy, more at home in the world of ideas than in the world of people and things.
Expansive and less impassioned, they unload their emotions as they go along.	Intense and passionate, they bottle up their emotions and guard them carefully as high explosives.
Typical weakness lies in a tendency toward intellectual superficiality, very conspicuous in extreme types.	Typical weakness lies in a tendency toward impracticality, very conspicuous in extreme types.
Health and wholesomeness depend upon a reasonable development of balancing introversion.	Health and wholesomeness depend upon a reasonable development of balancing extraversion.
Freud Darwin Roosevelt (both Theodore and Franklin Delano)	Jung Einstein Lincoln

Source of Figures 24–31: the notes of Katharine C. Briggs

CHAPTER 5

Effect of the SN Preference

ANYONE PREFERRING SENSING to intuition is interested primarily in actualities; anyone preferring intuition to sensing is mainly interested in possibilities.

This preference is entirely independent of the EI preference. Intuitives do not have to be introverts. Their possibilities can be external possibilities, pursued in the outer world of people and things. Sensing types do not have to be extraverts. They can be just as matter-of-fact in the world of ideas.

The sensing types, by definition, depend on their five senses for perception. Whatever comes directly from the senses is part of the sensing types' own experience and is therefore trustworthy. What comes from other people indirectly *through the spoken or written word* is less trustworthy. Words are merely symbols that have to be translated into reality before they mean anything, and therefore they carry less conviction than experience.

The intuitives are comparatively uninterested in sensory reports of things as they are. Instead, intuitives listen for the intuitions that come up from their unconscious with enticing visions of possibilities. As stated earlier, these contributions from the unconscious processes vary from the merest masculine "hunch" and "woman's intuition," through the whole range of original ideas, projects, enterprises, and inventions, to the crowning examples of creative art, religious inspiration, and scientific discovery.

The common factor in all these manifestations of intuition is a sort of ski jump—a soaring take-off from the known and established, ending in a swooping arrival at an advanced point, with the intervening steps apparently left out. Those steps are not really left out, of course; they are performed in and by the unconscious, often with extraordinary speed, and the result of the unconscious processes pops into the conscious mind with an effect of inspiration and certainty. To the intuitives, these inspirations are the breath of life. The only fields that interest intuitives are those that give inspiration some play. They abhor the routine because it leaves nothing for inspiration to accomplish.

Thus the innovator, the pioneer in thought or action, is likely to be an intuitive. In the early days of colonial America, the appeal of the New World's possibilities were probably felt so much more strongly by intuitives than by sensing types that it introduced a potent factor of selection. If the American colonies (and after them the Dominions) drew off a disproportionate share of the intuitives and left an unusually large majority of sensing types in England, some of the commonly attributed national characteristics might be explained. The solidity, conservatism, and dogged patience of the English, their love of custom and tradition, their unhurried addiction to afternoon tea and the long weekend belong to the sensing types, who know how to accept and value their world as it is. Our "American individualism," "Yankee ingenuity," and cult of "bigger and better" belong just as surely to the intuitives with their enthusiasm for what is just around the corner. The direction that the intuitives have imparted to our national life does not, however, mean that they are in the majority. Even in the United States the intuitives seem to make up only about one-fourth or less of the general population.

The proportion of intuitives varies widely from one educational level to another. It is particularly low among students in vocational and general high school courses, and at least twice as high in academic high school classes, and still higher in college, especially in very selective colleges. A sample of National Merit Finalists was 83 percent intuitive. (To compare various samples, see Chapter 3, Figures 3–23.) The preference for intuition *appears* to conduce to the pursuit of higher education, but the difference may be as much in interest as aptitude .

Whether an applicant is admitted to a given college may seem to rest entirely on the admissions committee's evaluation of the student's record, including grades and scholastic aptitude scores. Actually, for twelve years, the student has been casting a silent, unconscious vote whether to go to that or any other college. For example, after studying as hard as possible but without interest in academics, a student might not want four more years of school. This sentiment would be reflected in the student's grades. On the average, sensing children have less scholastic interest than intuitive children. (What might be done about this tendency is discussed in Chapter 13.)

Sensing children also make lower scores on the average than intuitive children on intelligence tests and scholastic aptitude tests. It would be grossly mistaken but easy to conclude that sensing types are less "intelligent"; such tests do not take into account the legitimate choice between two rival techniques for the application of intelligence to life.

The sensing child's native language is the reality spoken by the senses. The intuitive's native language is the word, the metaphor, the symbol, spoken by the unconscious. Most mental tests are of necessity couched in the intuitive's language. The sensing child has more translating to do, and translating takes time.

Although intelligence tests are usually speed tests for the sake of convenience, it is debatable whether speed has any rightful place in the basic concept of intelligence. Intuitives tend to define intelligence as "quickness of understanding" and so prejudge the case in their own favor, for intuition is very quick. The intuitive's technique is a lightning referral of the problem to the unconscious, which works very rapidly, and an immediate pounce upon the answer.

The sensing types are not in such close communication with their unconscious. They do not trust an answer that suddenly appears. They do not think it prudent to pounce. They tend to define intelligence as "soundness of understanding," a sure and solid agreement of conclusions with facts; and how is that possible until the facts have been considered? Therefore in reaching a conclusion they want to make sure of its soundness, like an engineer examining a bridge before deciding how much weight it can safely bear. They will not skim in reading, and they hate to have people skim in conversation. Believing that matters inferred are not as reliable as matters explicitly stated, they are annoyed when you leave things to their imagination. (Intuitives are often annoyed—if not actually bored—when you do not.)

Thus, a sensing child taking an intelligence test tends to read each question slowly and thoughtfully several times and, of course, answers fewer questions than the intuitive. Sensing people confirm this. An ISFJ, working in a personnel office that used the Type Indicator, was asked about her own technique for taking tests. She said, "Oh, I always read a question three or four times. I have to!" She does not have to in order to understand, but she does have to in order to be *satisfied* that she understands. So she goes slowly, and her slowness is the drawback. Some able sensing people manage to sacrifice their natural deliberation in taking tests, but it goes against their grain. An ISTJ psychologist, who had had an unbroken series of surprisingly low test scores until he came to his

Graduate Record Exams, recalls he was so disgusted with his performance that he decided he could do no worse if he "raced through like an idiot." For the first time in his life, he scored high.

The choice between the two rival techniques of perception has a profound effect upon school work from the very start. Sensing children just out of kindergarten, with no instinct for symbols, are not likely to divine for themselves that a letter means anything beyond what it obviously is—a shape on a page. If nobody explains to them what it means, they may still be seeing shapes on a page long after the intuitive children are seeing sounds, words, and meanings; and when they begin to read, they will seldom read for pleasure until they find a book containing facts they want to know.

Often the sensing children are equally betrayed in the field of arithmetic. Before they start school, they need to get a soundly quantitative notion of number so that they know *threeness* as a quality for which *three* is a handy symbol; *otherwise, in too many schools they will learn that "three" is a squiggle on the blackboard.* They have a good eye and they learn their squiggles thoroughly. Presently they are told that when a twisted line called *two* appears beneath another shape called *three*, they must remember to put at the bottom a more complicated figure called *five*. They generally have a good memory, and they learn that. With flash-cards and much drill, they learn by rote all the "addition facts" and "subtraction facts" about squiggles, but there is nothing *inherent* in the learning to make them suspect that the twisted lines *mean* anything. For many of these children, two-plus-three is entirely different from three-plus-two, and has to be learned separately.

The sensing children are accurate in simple computations as a rule, because they are more careful than the intuitives; but when they reach algebra or problems presented in words, many of them have difficulty in seeing *what* to compute. One twelve-year-old girl said of a percentage problem, "Here! I've done it all three ways, but I don't know which is right!" Most of the intuitive children, who understand symbols, recognize the meaning of figures in the beginning and are ready to work on the problems without too much difficulty. The contrast can make the sensing children feel stupid, which is discouraging.

Sensing types, of course, are not stupid at all—but someone should have shown them the significance of numbers before they were six years old. If they are given the meaning of numbers in a form that they comprehend from the start so that they understand what they are doing, they will enjoy the fact that two-plus-two *can be depended on* to make four.

They may even want to make a lifework of dealing with figures. Sensing types are sound and accurate and enjoy exactitude, so they make fine accountants, payroll administrators, navigators, and statisticians.

For sensing children to exercise their special gift of realism, they must have access to the facts and time to assimilate them. Whereas the intuitive children like to learn by insight, the sensing children prefer to learn by familiarization. The sensing types are most likely to shine in courses involving many solid facts, like history, geography, civics, or biology. They are at a corresponding disadvantage in subjects based on general principles. Often the trouble may be simply that the teacher has been too brief and abstract in referring to the principles and has passed over them so quickly that the sensing students have not had time to relate them to the facts. Physics, for example, can be a nightmare to the factually minded.

One case in point may be cited for its irony. An earnest and hardworking "B" student who wanted to be a doctor and was an excellent type for it, an ISFJ, flunked a pre-medical course because he could not keep up in physics with the engineers. Now he is a doctor and his patients do not care about the speed of his diagnosis, so long as it is sound. The very reliance upon sensing that made physics difficult is useful now. He is dealing with immediate realities—the rhythm of a heartbeat, the sound of breathing, the shade of flush or pallor—the myriad details a doctor must note and weigh. Touch, sight, and hearing must be his ultimate guides in applying either his own experience or the wisdom of his books. Research medicine, the medical school faculties, and the complex specialties need the intuitives; but as family doctors the sensing types come into their own, and their aptitude for physics has little if anything to do with their competence. Johns Hopkins University long ago recognized this discrepancy and instituted a special physics course for premedical students. The regular course had been disqualifying valued students.

When the time comes that educators take into account the SN preference and try to meet the divergent needs of students, beginning with kindergartners, there will be a much happier and more effective use of human resources. Young realists will no longer be penalized for their reliance on direct observation and first-hand experience—as Charles Darwin was in his boyhood, when his classical schoolmasters rated him below average in mental power.

A summary of the contrasting traits resulting from the SN preference is given here in parallel columns in Figure 25. These traits are most evident in the EP types, whose perceptive process is both *extraverted and dominant* and consequently most visible and least restrained. When the perceptive process is merely the auxiliary, it is subordinate to the judgment of the dominant process, and its manifestations tend to be more moderate.

Figure 25. Effect of the SN Preference

Sensing Types	**Intuitive Types**
Face life observantly, craving enjoyment.	Face life expectantly, craving inspiration.
Admit to consciousness every sense impression and are intensley aware of the external environment; they are observant at the expense of imagination.	Admit fully to consciousness only the sense impressions related to the current inspiration; they are imaginative at the expense of observation.
Are by nature pleasure lovers and consumers, loving life as it is and having a great capacity for enjoyment; they are in general contented.	Are by nature initiators, inventors, and promoters; having no taste for life as it is, and small capacity for living as it is, and small capacity for living in and enjoying the present, they are generally restless.
Desire chiefly to possess and enjoy, and being very observant, they are imitative, wanting to have what other people have and to do what other people do, and are very dependent upon their physical surroundings.	Desiring chiefly opportunities and possibilities, and being very imaginative, they are inventive and original, quite indifferent to what other people have and do, and are very independent of their physical surroundings.
Dislike intensely any and every occupation that requires the suppression of sensing, and are most reluctant to sacrifice present enjoyment to future gain or good.	Dislike intensely any and every occupation that necessitates sustained concentration on sensing, and are willing to sacrifice the present to a large extent since they neither live in it nor particularly enjoy it.
Prefer the art of living in the present to the satisfactions of enterprise and achievement.	Prefer the joy of enterprise and achievement and pay little or no attention to the art of living in the present.
Contribute to the public welfare by their support of every form of enjoyment and recreation, and every variety of comfort, luxury, and beauty.	Contribute to the public welfare by their inventiveness, initiative, enterprise, and powers of inspired leadership in every direction of human interest.
Are always in danger of being frivolous, unless balance is attained through development of a judging process.	Are always in danger of being fickle, changeable, and lacking in persistence, unless balance is attained through development of a judging process.

CHAPTER 6

Effect of the TF Preference

THINKING AND FEELING are rival instruments of decision. Both are reasonable and internally consistent, but each works by its own standards. Jolande Jacobi (1968) says that thinking evaluates from the viewpoint "true–false" and feeling from the viewpoint "agreeable–disagreeable." This sounds like a thinker's formulation. "Agreeable" is too pale a word for the rich personal worth of a feeling evaluation.

The important point to recognize is that each kind of judgment has its appropriate field. To use feeling where thinking is called for can be as great a mistake as to use thinking where feeling is needed.

Thinking is essentially impersonal. Its goal is objective truth, independent of the personality and wishes of the thinker or anyone else. A seventeen-year-old introverted thinker, speculating on the method and purpose of the Creation, summed it up, "I don't care *what* the truth turns out to be—but I want it to hang together." So long as the problems are impersonal, like those involved in building a bridge or interpreting a statute, proposed solutions can and should be judged from the standpoint "true–false," and thinking is the better instrument.

But the moment the subject is people instead of things or ideas—and some voluntary cooperation from those people is needed—the impersonal approach is less successful. People (even thinkers) do not like to be viewed impersonally and relegated to the status of "objects." Human motives are notably personal. Therefore, in the sympathetic handling of people where personal values are important, feeling is the more effective instrument.

To thinkers, the idea of evaluating by means of feeling sounds flighty, unreliable, and uncontrolled, but thinkers are no judges of feeling. They naturally judge all feeling by their own, and theirs is relatively undeveloped and unreliable. When feeling is well developed, it is a stable instrument for discriminating the worth of personal values, selecting as guiding stars those values that rank highest, and subordinating the lesser to the greater. When feeling is extraverted and directed upon other people, it not only recognizes their personal values but manages to convey its own.

Thus, in teaching, in acting and the other arts, in oratory and in that humbler branch of persuasion called salesmanship, in the relations of the clergy to their congregations, in family life, in social contacts, and in any sort of counseling, *it is feeling which serves as the bridge between one human being and another*.

The TF preference is the only one that shows a marked sex difference. The proportion of feeling types appears to be substantially higher among women than among men. This difference in the frequencies of the types for men and women has led to much generalization about the sexes. Women have been assumed to be less logical, more tender-hearted, more tactful, more social, less analytical, and more inclined to take things personally. All these are feeling traits. Feeling types (of either sex) will tend to have them. Thinking types (of either sex) will not. The generalization tends to pass over the women with thinking and the men with feeling, partly because types that do not fit the stereotypes have often learned the art of protective coloration.

The merits of the thinker's logical approach to life are so obvious and so well known that it has not seemed necessary to discuss them here. (They are treated in some detail in the individual descriptions of the thinking types in Chapter 9.) But it should never be assumed that thinkers have a monopoly on all worthwhile mental activity. They do not even have a monopoly on thinking. Just as thinkers may attain, on occasion, a very useful supplementary development of feeling that does not interfere with their thinking judgments, so too the feeling types may sometimes enlist their thinking to find the logical reasons needed to win a thinker's acceptance of a conclusion they have already reached by way of feeling. Before the publication of a cherished piece of work, undertaken from motives of feeling and carried out intuitively, thinking may be used to check for possible flaws and fallacies.

Conventional measures of mental ability, such as intelligence tests and scholarship, show some of the very highest records belong to INFP and INFJ types, who relegate thinking to last place or next to last. The preference for thinking appears to have far less intellectual effect than the preference for intuition, even in some technical fields, such as scientific research, where its influence was expected to be most important.

It would seem, therefore, that the mark of a thinker is not so much the possession of greater mental powers but having them run on a different track. Thinkers are at their best with the impersonal, and they are the most able to handle things that need to be done impersonally. The judge and the surgeon, for example, tend to rule out all personal considerations. One famous surgeon was so impersonal that his wife could not even focus his attention on his own children unless she took them to his office.

Finally, thinking is not always first-class thinking. Its product is no better than the facts it started with (and they were acquired by perception of unknown quality) and no better than the logic employed. When a person who reportedly described *logic* as an organized way of going wrong with confidence, he voiced the distrust of the out-and-out intuitives and the feeling types for such a cut-and-dried method of decision. When feeling types know that they value an idea or a person or a course of action, a thinker's argument designed to confute that value leaves them cold. The thinker's judgment could be wrong! Thinkers often contradict each other, each one claiming, "This is truth." The feeling type need only say, "This is valuable to me."

The summary in Figure 26 differentiates the people in the outer columns of the Type Table from those in the middle columns. The traits mentioned are most evident in the EJ types, whose judging process is both extraverted and dominant and consequently most visible and emphatic. When the judging process is merely the auxiliary, it is subordinate to the perceptions of the dominant process and its manifestations tend to be more moderate.

Figure 26. Effect of the TF Preference

Thinking Types	Feeling Types
Value logic above sentiment.	Value sentiment above logic.
Are usually impersonal, being more interested in things than in human relationships.	Are usually personal, being more interested in people than in things.
If forced to choose between truthfulness and tactfulness, will usually be truthful.	If forced to choose between tactfulness and truthfulness, will usually be tactful.
Are stronger in executive ability than in the social arts.	Are stronger in the social arts than in executive ability.
Are likely to question the conclusions of other people on principle—believing them probably wrong.	Are likely to agree with those around them, thinking as other people think, believing them probably right.
Naturally brief and businesslike, they often seem to lack friendliness and sociability without knowing or intending it.	Are naturally friendly, whether sociable or not, they find it difficult to be brief and businesslike.
Are usually able to organize facts and ideas into a logical sequence that states the subject, makes the necessary points, comes to a conclusion, and stops there without repetition.	Usually find it hard to know where to start a statement or in what order to present what they have to say. May therefore ramble and repeat themselves, with more detail than a thinker wants or thinks necessary.
Suppress, undervalue, and ignore feeling that is incompatible with the thinking judgments.	Suppress, undervalue, and ignore thinking that is offensive to the feeling judgments.
Contribute to the welfare of society by the intellectual criticism of its habits, customs, and beliefs, by the exposure of wrongs, solution of problems, and the support of science and research for the enlargement of human knowledge and understanding.	Contribute to the welfare of society by their loyal support of good works and those movements, generally regarded as good by the community, which they feel correctly about and so can serve effectively.
Are found more often among men than women and when married to a feeling type naturally become guardian of the spouse's neglected and unreliable thinking.	Are found more often among women than men and, when married to a thinking type, frequently become guardian of the spouse's neglected and harrassed feelings.

CHAPTER 7

Effect of the JP Preference

THE JUDGING TYPES believe that life should be willed and decided, while the perceptive types regard life as something to be experienced and understood. Thus, judging types like to settle things, or at least to have things settled, whereas perceptive types prefer to keep their plans and opinions as open as possible so that no valuable experience or enlightenment will be missed. The contrast in their lives is quite evident.

Judgment is eternally coming to conclusions—with the finality the word implies. Judgment really *likes* to dispose of things, even without the spur of necessity. Frequently judging types settle not only what they are to do themselves, but what others are to do. Given a little provocation, they settle what others are to think. The person who says "What you ought to do..." ten minutes after meeting someone new is a marked judging type.

Less-marked judging types think to themselves what someone else ought to do, but suppress the impulse to speak out. Perceptive types do not even think it. They would rather hear about what a person *is* doing. Two immortal examples of perception are Kipling's Rikki-tikki-tavi, whose motto was "run and find out," and the insatiably curious Elephant's Child who went around getting spanked for asking "why?"

Such inexhaustible interest in "what?" and "why?" does not conduce to finality. The perceptive types do not come to conclusions until they must—and sometimes not even then. Being cognizant of how many factors are involved and how much is still unknown, they are rather horrified at the eagerness of the judging types to decide a matter. The saying that "a bad decision is better than none" makes sense only to a judging type. Perceptive types always hope that they can solve the problem simply by understanding it better, by "seeing to the bottom of it" if they are intuitives or by "seeing it from all sides" if they are sensing types. Often they can. In such cases they are hardly conscious of

69

judgment; the solution has been latent there in the situation and they have eventually "seen" what was the thing to do.

Of course, the perceptive types still need judgment. Their perception should be *supported* by an adequately developed judging process. Otherwise, they will drift downwind like a sailboat with its centerboard up. *It takes judgment* (either thinking or feeling will do) *to give continuity of purpose and supply a standard by which to criticize and govern one's own actions.*[7]

At the other extreme, judging types with insufficient perception have no "give" or cooperation in them. If they lack an adequately developed perceptive process, they will be narrow, rigid, and incapable of seeing any point of view except their own. This characteristic of the relentlessly judging individual is recognized in the word *prejudice*—a prejudgment impervious to perception.

Furthermore, if thinking or feeling types lack perceptions of their own, they will be obliged to rely on the forms of judgment in default of content. They will accept the forms current in their environment: Thinkers will depend on the formulas and accepted principles; feeling types will adopt the attitudes of approval and disapproval. But they will apply these mechanically, with no genuine insight into the particular situation. *It takes perception* (either sensing or intuition will do) *to supply understanding, open-mindedness, and the first-hand knowledge of life needed to keep judgment itself from being blind.*

Thus well-balanced individuals must always have perception to support their judgment, and judgment to support their perception. They will still retain their basic preference and the qualities it gives. The gifts of judgment include:

- *System in doing things.* It is natural for a judging type to decide what is the best way of doing a thing and then consistently do it that way. The thinking process tries for the most logical method; the feeling process for the most pleasing, suitable, or proper method.

- *Order in possessions.* It is a judging sentiment that order is Heaven's first law. Thinking types believe in orderliness for utilitarian reasons. TJ types may have everything inside their bureau drawers neatly classified in boxes but not concern themselves with the state of the bureau top; FJ types, more esthetically inclined, are almost certain to have the top neat, too.

■ *The planned life.* Order applied to one's activities means programs and schedules. The judging types decide in advance what they intend to accomplish, and they make careful and sometimes very long-range plans. FJs tend to have the fullest schedules because of their many social activities.

■ *Sustained effort.* Having once decided to do a thing, the judging types continue to do it. This application of willpower results in impressive accomplishments. The tortoise in the race was certainly a judging type. The hare, because he liked to operate in tremendous spurts, was probably an extraverted intuitive but lacked adequate judgment.

■ *Decisiveness.* Not everyone who lives in the judging attitude enjoys the actual making of decisions. Some simply dislike to have things remain undecided. These are more likely to be feeling types than thinkers.

■ *Exercise of authority.* The judging types want to see other people conform to their standards and are usually glad to advise them. The TJ people often have better executive and organizing abilities, but where the rules are firmly laid down, the FJs can be very good at gentle enforcement. Of 124 school administrators cited by von Fange (1961), 86 percent were J.

■ *Settled opinions.* Judging types usually know what they think about everything they consider worth thinking about.

■ *Acceptance of routine.* Acceptance of routine is put last because any marked development of intuition is apt to cancel it out, but judging types with sensing seem able to take routine more philosophically than any of the other types.

Among the gifts of perception are:

■ *Spontaneity.* Spontaneity is the ability to take whole-heartedly the experience or enlightenment of the present moment, even though some intended thing goes undone. Perceptive types believe it can be more important to go and look at a bird's nest that the children have found, or to take time out to help hunt up the answer to a question, or to listen to a confidence with one's whole heart, than to have a meal on time.

- *Open-mindedness*. Perception involves a certain hospitality of mind, a willingness to admit to consideration of new facts, ideas, and proposals, even though they involve the reopening of decisions or opinions. The perceptive types leave many decisions and opinions standing wide open in expectation of new information.

- *Understanding*. Perception is applied to people in order to understand their point of view rather than to pass judgment on their actions. Parents who take the perceptive attitude with their children whenever possible will be entrusted with many more confidences than parents who have an immediate (and usually critical) opinion about everything they are told. The comparatively rare pronouncements of the perceptive parents will be accorded more respect, because the parents will have done enough listening to appreciate the situation.

   A *generally* perceptive attitude is perfectly consistent with firm parental discipline. Discipline is needed to enforce the fundamentals, preferably a few fundamentals. If children observe those faithfully, they are acceptable members of society, and just like grown-ups, they are entitled to be spared a running commentary on their every act.

- *Tolerance*. The "live and let live" attitude arises partly from reluctance to settle things for other people and partly from perceptive recognition that there can be a variety of legitimate standards. Tolerance grows dangerous only when carried to the extreme of condoning actual *lack* of standards in some essential field.

- *Curiosity*. One of the liveliest gifts of the perceptive types is the expectation that what they do not yet know will be interesting. Curiosity leads them into many byways of knowledge and experience and into amassing astonishing stores of information. It also wards off boredom, as it finds something of interest in almost any situation.

- *Zest for experience*. Another expectation of the perceptives is that what they have not yet done is going to be interesting. They may refuse a new experience on grounds of taste or principle or in favor of a more compelling attraction, but seldom because it is "not worth doing," as the judging types say.

- *Adaptability.* The perceptive handles a difficulty by adapting the available means for the achievement of the essential ends. One very perceptive woman cherishes a compliment from her judging husband on how effectively she reassembles the fragments of a situation when something unforeseen upsets all the existing arrangements. Because she is never tied to the old plan, she is free to improvise a new one to meet the altered conditions, and *enjoys doing it.*

In considering the qualities listed above, readers may have difficulty evaluating their own JP preference because of an inconsistency between what they feel they should do, what they actually do, and what they naturally tend to do. It is the natural tendency that reveals the basic preference. A person's idea of what is right may be an acquired ideal, borrowed from another type, and the person's actual behavior may reflect a somewhat uncongenial good habit learned from parents or accepted because of the person's own dogged efforts.

It is important, especially for introverts, to remember that the JP preference applies to a person's customary attitude toward the outer world. What shows in most casual contacts with other people (and governs the JP index on the Type Indicator) is the extraverted process, the one usually relied on for the conduct of outer life. For extraverts, it is the same as the dominant process; for introverts it is not.

Thus, in an introvert the preference for the judging attitude in outer matters may be quite evident, even obvious, but it is not final. The judging process used in the outer world is actually subordinate to the introverted dominant process (which is a perceptive one) and operates subject to the requirements of that favorite perceptive process. For example, if thinking is the extraverted process, it will conduct things with logic and decisiveness, but logic will not be allowed to hamper the inner perception.

Similarly, in an introvert whose preference for the perceptive attitude is ordinarily obvious, this perceptiveness is actually subordinate to an introverted judging process (thinking or feeling) and must serve the ultimate values and principles determined by the judging process. A very perceptive introvert student was surprised when she was voted "most decisive" in her high school class. The vote was taken soon after several issues had arisen that touched feeling values she held fundamental. Her inner certainty had overruled her habitual outer perceptiveness, and she had defended her position on all the issues.

Some differences resulting from the JP preference are compared in Figure 27. In general, these characteristics differentiate extraverts in the bottom row of the Type Table from those in the third row. They also differentiate introverts in the top row from those in the second row, with certain exceptions due to the special role of the introvert's dominant process.

Figure 27. Effect of the JP Preference

Judging Types[8]	Perceptive Types[9]
Are more decisive than curious.	Are more curious than decisive.
Live according to plans, standards, and customs not easily or lightly set aside, to which the situation of the moment must, if possible, be made to conform.	Live according to the situation of the moment and adjust themselves easily to the accidental and the unexpected.
Make a very definite choice among life's possibilities, but may not appreciate or utilize unplanned, unexpected, and incidental happenings.	Are frequently masterful in their handling of the unplanned, unexpected, and incidental, but may not make an effective choice among life's possibilities.
Being rational, they depend upon reasoned judgments, their own or borrowed from someone else, to protect them from unnecessary undesirable experiences.	Being empirical, they depend on their readiness for anything and everything to bring them a constant flow of new experience—much or more than they can digest or use.
Like to have matters settled and decided as promptly as possible, so that they will know what is going to happen and can plan for it and be prepared for it.	Like to keep decisions open as long as possible before doing anything irrevocable, because they don't know nearly enough about it yet.
Think or feel that they know what other people ought to do about almost everything, and are not averse to telling them.	Know what other people are doing, and are interested to see how it comes out.
Take real pleasure in getting something finished, out of the way, and off their minds.	Take great pleasure in starting something new, until the newness wears off.
Are inclined to regard the perceptive types as aimless drifters.	Are inclined to regard the judging types as only half-alive.
Aim to be right.	Aim to miss nothing.
Are self-regimented, purposeful, and exacting.	Are flexible, adaptable, and tolerant.

CHAPTER 8

Extraverted and Introverted Forms of the Processes Compared

THE EFFECT OF each of the four preferences—between introversion and extraversion, between sensing and intuiting, between thinking and feeling, and between judging and perceiving—have been discussed in the preceding chapters. *In combination*, the four preferences determine type, but the traits that result from each preference do not combine to influence an individual's personality by simple *addition* of characteristics; instead, the traits result from the interaction of the preferences.

The effect of the interaction of the preferred processes is made apparent when the extraverted form of a particular process—thinking, feeling, sensing, or intuition—is compared with the introverted form of the same process. The four figures that make up the balance of this chapter, Figures 28–31, present contrasting pairs of sentences describing the extraverted and introverted forms of thinking, feeling, sensing, and intuition. The comparisons presented in the figures, which were drawn by Katharine C. Briggs during her initial study of *Psychological Types*, include the effects of extraversion and introversion on the kinds of information a particular process uses or suppresses; the strengths, the weaknesses, and the goals of the four processes discussed; how each of the processes expresses itself; and so on.

Figure 28. Comparison of Extraverted and Introverted Thinking

Extraverted Thinking	Introverted Thinking
Is fed from objective data—facts and borrowed ideas.	Is fed from subjective and unconscious roots—archetypes.
Depends upon the facts of experience and regards the abstract idea as unsubstantial and of negligible importance.	Depends upon the abstract idea as the decisive factor, and values facts chiefly as illustrative proofs of the idea.
Relies on facts outside of the thinker, which are more decisive than the thinking itself, for soundness and value.	Relies on the thinker's powers of observation and appreciation and use of the inner wealth of inherited experience for soundness and value.
Has as its goal the solution of practical problems, discovery and classification of facts, criticism and modification of generally accepted ideas, planning of programs, and developing of formulas.	Has as its goal formulating questions, creating theories, opening up of prospects, yielding insight, and finally, seeing how external facts fit into the framework of the idea or theory it has created.
Dwells upon the details of the concrete case, including irrelevancies.	Seizes upon the similarities of the concrete case, dismissing irrelevancies.
Has a tendency to multiply facts until their meaning is smothered and thinking paralyzed.	Has a tendency to neglect facts or to coerce them into agreement with the idea, selecting only those which support the idea.
Consists of a succession of concrete representations that are set in motion not so much by an inner thought activity as by the changing stream of sense perceptions.	Consists of an inner thought activity, tied loosely if at all to the stream of sense impressions, which are dimmed by the vividness of the stream of inner impressions.

Figure 29. Comparison of Extraverted and Introverted Feeling

Extraverted Feeling	**Introverted Feeling**
Is determined chiefly by the objective factor and serves to make the individual feel correctly, that is, conventionally, under all circumstances.	Is determined chiefly by the subjective factor and serves as a guide to the emotional acceptance or rejection of various aspects of life.
Adapts the individual to the objective situation.	Adapts the objective situation to the individual by the simple process of excluding or ignoring the unacceptable.
Depends wholly upon the ideals, conventions, and customs of the environment, and is extensive rather than deep.	Depends upon abstract feeling— ideals such as love, patriotism, religion, and loyalty, and is deep and passionate rather than extensive.
Finds soundness and value outside of the individual in the collective ideals of the community, which are usually accepted without question.	Finds soundness and value inside one's self from one's own inner wealth and powers of appreciation and abstraction.
Has as goal the formation and maintenance of easy and harmonious emotional relationships with other people.	Has as goal the fostering and protection of an intense inner emotional life, and, so far as possible, the outer fulfillment and realization of the inner ideal.
Expresses itself easily and so shares itself with others, creating and arousing similar feeling and establishing warm sympathy and understanding.	May be too overpowering to be expressed at all, creating a false appearance of coldness to the point of indifference, and be completely misunderstood.
Has a tendency to suppress the personal standpoint entirely, and presents the danger of becoming a feeling personality, giving the effect of insincerity and pose.	Has a tendency to find no objective fulfillment or realization, or outlet— for expression, and presents the danger of living upon sentiment, illusion, and self-pity.

Figure 30. Comparison of Extraverted and Introverted Sensing

Extraverted Sensing	Introverted Sensing
Suppresses as far as possible the subjective element of the sense impression.	Suppresses as far as possible the objective element of the sense impression.
Values the object sensed rather than the subjective impression, of which the individual may hardly be aware.	Values the subjective impression released by the object rather than the object itself, of which the individual may hardly be aware.
Sees things photographically, the impression being one of concrete reality and nothing more. The "primrose by a river's brim" is simply a primrose.	Sees things highly colored by the subjective factor, the impression being merely suggested by the object and coming out of the unconscious in the form of some meaning or significance.
Leads to concrete enjoyment, seizing very fully the momentary and manifest existence of things, and that only.	Leads to ideas, through the activation of archetypes, seizing the background of the physical world rather than its surface.
Develops attention that is riveted by the strongest stimulus, which invariably becomes the center of interest, so that life seems wholly under the influence of accidental outer happenings.	Develops attention that is very selective, guided wholly by the inner constellation of interests, so that it is impossible to predict what outer stimulus will catch and hold attention.
Develops a pleasure-loving outer self, very rich in undigested experience and unclassified knowledge of uninterpreted facts.	Develops an extremely eccentric and individual inner self, which sees things other people do not see, and may appear very irrational.
Must be balanced by introverting judgment, or it makes a shallow, wholly empirical personality, with many superstitions and no morality except collective conventions and taboos.	Must be balanced by extraverting judgment, or it makes a silent, inaccessible personality, wholly uncommunicative, with no conversation except conventional banalities about the weather and other collective interests.

Figure 31. Comparison of Extraverted and Introverted Intuition

Extraverted Intuition	Introverted Intuition
Uses the inner understanding in the interests of the objective situation.	Uses the objective situation in the interests of the inner understanding.
Regards the immediate situation as a prison from which escape is urgently necessary and aims to escape by means of some sweeping change in the objective situation.	Regards the immediate situation as a prison from which escape is urgently necessary and aims to escape through some sweeping change in the subjective understanding of the objective situation.
Is wholly directed upon outer objects, searching for emerging possibilities, and will sacrifice all else for such possibilities when found.	Receives its impetus from outer objects but is never arrested by external possibilities, being occupied rather by searching out new angles for viewing and understanding life.
May be artistic, scientific, mechanical, inventive, industrial, commercial, social, political, or adventurous.	May be creative in any field: artistic, literary, scientific, inventive, philosophical, or religious.
Finds self-expression natural and easy.	Finds self-expression difficult.
Finds its greatest value in the promotion and initiation of new enterprises.	Finds its greatest value lies in the interpretation of life and the promotion of understanding.
Requires the development of balancing judgment not only for the criticism and evaluation of the intuitive enthusiasms but also to hold it to the completion of its various activities.	Requires the development of balancing judgment not only for the criticism and evaluation of intuitive understanding but to enable it to impart its visions to others and bring them to practical usefulness in the world.

Both are characterized by habitual expectancy;
both have quick understanding.

CHAPTER 9

Descriptions
of the Sixteen Types

OF THE SIXTEEN specific types that result from the various combinations of the preferences, each is the product of its dominant process, extraverted or introverted as the case may be, and modified by the nature of its auxiliary. (The modification is especially marked in the introvert types, whose auxiliary is mainly responsible for their outer behavior.) When statements made about a type are thought of in terms of cause and effect, the characteristics of each type are easier to remember and look for.

The descriptions do not include all the traits arising from each preference, which were discussed in Chapters 4–8. Every introvert type is expected to have the general introvert characteristics. To repeat them each time would only tend to obscure the special characteristics of the particular variety of introvert.

Critics of Jung's theory have often charged that introversion is not a unitary trait: There are "too many kinds of introverts." Introversion is not a trait, but a basic disposition or orientation. In each of the eight kinds of introverts, this orientation takes on a different aspect as a necessary result of the other preferences involved.

Each of the following descriptions deals with two types that differ only in the choice of the auxiliary process. The first description considers the two extraverted thinking types, ESTJ and ENTJ, what they have in common, and the ways in which they differ. The next description deals with the two introverted thinking types, ISTP and INTP, in the same fashion. Then extraverted and introverted feeling types, extraverted and introverted sensing types, and extraverted and introverted intuitives are discussed.

As might be expected, the greatest similarity between an extravert type and an introvert type occurs when the two types differ only on EI. They will then have the same combination of perception and judgment, and their outer lives will be shaped by the same extraverted process. The resemblances are likely to be most marked in daily living, and less marked when something very important is in question and the introvert's dominant process takes over.

The Shadow Side

The descriptions are designed to apply to each type at its best, as exemplified by normal, well-balanced, well-adjusted, happy, and effective people. So the basic description assumes good development of both the dominant and auxiliary processes. Actually the types come in widely different states of development. If the auxiliary process is undeveloped, the person will lack balance between judgment and perception, and also between extraversion and introversion. If the dominant process is also undeveloped, there will not be much left of the type except its weaknesses.

Well-developed or not, everyone has a *shadow side*. Just as the conscious personality is the product of the best-developed processes, the *shadow* is the product of the least-developed part, which a person rejects and disowns. The shadow uses relatively childish and primitive kinds of judgment and perception, not intentionally in the service of conscious aims, but all on its own in an escape from the conscious personality and in defiance of conscious standards.

The results are usually regrettable. Acts of which a person says afterwards, "I don't know how I came to do that. I didn't mean to!" are usually the work of the shadow, and so are other regrettable things that a person may not even be aware of having done. The irascible Professor Henry Higgins insisted that he was "a very quiet man."

It is well to understand the shadow, as it explains some curious contradictions in people. If a person's apparent preferences indicate a given type, yet he or she has behaved in a way wholly alien to the type in question, consider the quality of the act. If it was inferior to the person's usual standard, there may have been a shadow at work.

A person's type is the product of conscious orientation to life: habitual, purposeful ways of using one's mind—habitual because they seem good and interesting and trustworthy. The shadow is something that happens when a person isn't looking.

Some introverts pay so little conscious attention to extraverting that they achieve little or no development of their *extraverted* auxiliary process. Their extraversion will be largely unconscious and their shadow processes may be more apparent than their conscious personalities. A woman completing the Type Indicator for her extremely introverted ISFJ husband as she sees him, may make him an ISTJ, missing the feeling he does not express, and reporting instead the unconscious, inferior, and critical thinking of his shadow side.

Extraverted Thinking Types
ESTJ and ENTJ

- Are analytical and impersonal

- May be executive, legal, technical, or interested in reform

- Organize the facts—and everything else within reach

- Are decisive, logical, strong in reasoning power

- Aim to govern their own conduct and other people's in accordance with thought-out conclusions

- Value truth in the form of fact, formula, and method

- Have an emotional life that is accidental

- Have a social life that is incidental

Extraverted thinkers use their thinking to run as much of the world as may be theirs to run. They are in their element whenever the outer situation needs to be organized, criticized, or regulated. Ordinarily they enjoy deciding what ought to be done and giving the appropriate orders to ensure that it will be done. They abhor confusion, inefficiency, half measures, anything that is aimless and ineffective. Often they are crisp disciplinarians, who know how to be tough when the situation calls for toughness.

This might be called the standard executive type. There are other kinds of executives, some of them brilliantly successful. But it is doubtful whether any other type so *enjoys* being an executive, or works so hard to get to be one. Sometimes at an early age, a child of this type, with systematic purpose and natural interest in running things, becomes, popularity aside, the leader of the school class.

Much of the extraverted thinkers' effectiveness stems from their willingness to issue as strict orders to themselves as to anyone else. They stake out their objectives well in advance and put a lot of systematic effort into reaching them on schedule. At their best, they turn an unsparing eye upon their own conduct and revise whatever does not come up to standard.

Extraverted thinkers naturally prefer the judging attitude, and they act forcefully upon the basis of their judgments, whether well-founded or not. One of them wrote me: "Say something about the almost irresistible urge to *make* decisions, just for their own sake. Under this urge I will not only make quick and accurate decisions *in my own field* but will tend to make equally quick but *faulty* decisions in a strange field, just because I'm intent on decisions and do not take time to perceive the facts fully."

Extraverted thinkers must develop a good perceptive auxiliary to give them grounds for judgments and must learn to suspend judgment long enough to give perception a chance. This might be difficult, but the rewards are substantial. Not only will better perception make their judgments sounder, but if they use it to see other points of view, it will help them in human relations, where they may well need help.

Extraverted thinkers construct a code of rules embodying their basic judgments about the world. They aim to live by those rules, and consider that others should as well. Any change in their ways requires a conscious change in the rules. If their perception is not good enough to show them, from time to time, how their rules should be broadened, the code will be so narrow and rigid that it becomes a tyranny not only to the thinkers but also to those around them, especially their families. Everything that conforms to the rules will be right; everything that violates them will be wrong; and everything not covered by them will be unimportant. They will become, as Jung puts it, "a world-law whose realization must be achieved at all times and seasons.... [Anyone] who refuses to obey is wrong—he is resisting the world-law, and is, therefore, unreasonable, immoral and without a conscience" (1923, p. 435).

The basic mistake here is the infliction of one's own judgment on other people. Judging types should use their judgment on themselves, not on others. Thinking judgments are usually harder on the person judged than feeling judgments, because thinking is naturally critical. It analyzes, decides that things would be better if they were different, and usually says so, whereas feeling judgments tend to be complimentary part of the time. Feeling enjoys appreciating things. That may be too much to expect of thinkers in whom feeling is the least developed process, but thinkers can put it into their rules that from time to time they will use perception to see what there is about a person to appreciate—and mention it.

Against that background, any suggestions can be carried out with better grace than would otherwise be the case. Everyone likes to be treated perceptively, but it is especially important with subordinates, who cannot fight for their own viewpoints, and with children, husbands, and wives, who can do so only at the expense of family peace.

There is another reason why the thinkers should, for their own sake, practice the perceptive attitude. If they let thinking judgment dominate their every waking moment, their feeling will be too suppressed to be of any use to them. It may even acutely embarrass them at times by unexpected explosions of temper which consciously they would never "think" of committing. If they cultivate perception, however, by now and then turning off their thinking judgment, they give feeling a constructive outlet before it reaches the boiling point.

Extraverted thinkers are convinced by reasoning, and when they are convinced, that is quite an accomplishment, because when they decide to do something, it gets done.

Extraverted Thinking Supported by Sensing

ESTJs look at the world with sensing rather than intuition; hence, they are most interested in the realities perceived by their five senses, so they tend to be matter-of-fact and practical, receptive and retentive of factual detail, tolerant of routine, deft at mechanical things, realistic, and concerned with the here and now. Their thinking process appears deliberate, because it often is actual thinking, rather than the shortcut that is frequently furnished by intuition.

The curiosity of an ESTJ is stirred mainly by new things that appeal directly to the senses—new objects, gadgets or contrivances, new physical activities, new people, new houses, new food, and new scenery. New things that cannot be grasped through the senses—abstract ideas and theories—seem less real and are much less acceptable. Anything intangible is rather distasteful, as it undermines the security of a factual world in which people can be sure of their judgments.

The ESTJs solve problems by expertly applying and adapting past experience. They like work where they can achieve immediate, visible, and tangible results. They have a natural bent for business and industry, production and construction. They enjoy administration and getting things organized and done. Executives of this type prefer to base plans and decisions on established facts and procedures; they do not listen to their own intuition very much, and may need an intuitive around to point out the value of new ideas.

This is perhaps the most traditionally "masculine" type and includes more men than any other.

Extraverted Thinking Supported by Intuition

ENTJs look at the world with intuition rather than sensing, so they are mainly interested in the possibilities beyond the present, obvious, or known. Intuition heightens their intellectual interest, curiosity about new ideas (whether immediately useful or not), tolerance for theory, taste for complex problems, insight, vision, and concern for long-range possibilities and consequences.

ENTJs are seldom content in a job that makes no demand on intuition. They need problems to solve and are likely to be expert at finding new solutions. Their interest is in the broad picture, however, not in detailed procedures or facts.

Executives of this type are likely to surround themselves with other intuitives, because they like people who are quick on the uptake, with minds that work in the same fashion as their own, but they do well to have at least one good sensing type on their staff to keep them from overlooking relevant facts and important details.

Introverted Thinking Types
ISTP and INTP

- Are analytical and impersonal

- Are interested primarily in the underlying principles

- Are organized in relation to concepts and ideas (if INTP) or facts (if ISTP)—but *not* people or situations, unless of necessity

- Are perceptive, not dominating, as the decisiveness of the thinking usually shows only in intellectual matters

- Are outwardly quiet, reserved, detached, perhaps even aloof except with intimates

- Are inwardly absorbed in the current analysis or problem

- Are inclined toward shyness, especially when young, as the chief interests of introverted thinking are little help in small talk or social contacts

Introverted thinkers use their thinking to analyze the world, not to run it. Relying on thinking makes them logical, impersonal, objectively critical, not likely to be convinced by anything except reasoning. As introverts, they focus their thinking on the principles underlying things rather than on the things themselves. Because it is hard to switch their thinking from ideas to details of daily living, they lead their outer lives mainly with their preferred perceptive process, which makes them detachedly curious and quite adaptable—until one of their ruling principles is violated, at which point they stop adapting.

They are likely to be persevering and independent of external circumstances to a marked degree, with a singleness of purpose that subordinates the social and emotional aspects of life to some long-term achievement of the mind. They may have difficulty in conveying their conclusions to the rest of the world and getting these accepted or even understood. Jung says the introverted thinker "will hardly ever go out of his way to win anyone's appreciation of his ideas.... He merely exposes them, and is often extremely annoyed when they fail to thrive on their own account" (1923, p. 486).

Introverted thinking applied to mathematics can be seen in Einstein; applied to philosophy, in Kant; applied to world affairs, in Woodrow Wilson; and applied to psychology, in Jung. In the industrial field, the introverted thinker's job should be to work out the needed principles underlying a problem or operation. Then other types can go ahead and do the operating. A sweeping application of the principles underlying mass production may be seen in the achievements of Henry Ford. (Ford always took great pains to preserve his independence of action and spare himself the necessity of converting others to his plans.)

To be effective, the introverted thinkers *must* have a good auxiliary process to supply perception in support of their thinking. If neither their sensing nor their intuition is serviceably developed, they will suffer a general deficit of perception, so that their thinking will not have enough to think about and consequently will be barren and unproductive. The lack of an adequate auxiliary process will leave them short on extraversion, too. They will have inadequate relationship to the outside world, even by introvert standards.

The least-developed process of the introverted thinkers inevitably is extraverted feeling. They are not apt to know, unless told, what matters emotionally to another person, but they can and should act on the principle that people do care about having their merits appreciated and their point of view respectfully considered. Both the working life and the personal life of the introverted thinkers will go better if they take the trouble to do two simple things: Say an appreciative word when praise is honestly due, and mention the points on which they agree with another person *before* they bring up the points on which they disagree.

With introverted thinkers, as with all introverts, the choice of the auxiliary process makes a great difference and colors the outward personality. In the ISTP combination, sensing will lend realism, matter-of-factness, sometimes an unexpected gift of fun for its own sake, often an interest in sports and outdoor recreation in general. In the INTP combination, intuition will lend subtlety, imagination, and a liking for projects and occupations demanding ingenuity.

Choice of the auxiliary process also affects the *use* that will be made of the dominant process, because the kind of perception employed determines in large part what elements of the outer world will be brought to the attention of the ruling thinking. If sensing makes the selection, the material presented will be more tangible and concrete, often involving mechanics or statistics but in any case factual. If intuition does the choosing, the material will be more theoretical and abstract, giving scope for the exercise of insight and originality.

Introverted Thinking Supported by Sensing

ISTPs have a vested interest in practical and applied science, especially in the field of mechanics. Of all the processes, sensing provides for the greatest understanding of the visible and tangible properties of matter, how it behaves, what you can and cannot do with it. People of this type are likely to be good with their hands, which is a genuine asset in the practical application of scientific principles.

With nontechnical interests, the ISTPs can use general principles to bring order out of confused data and meaning out of unorganized facts. The capacity of sensing to absorb fact and detail can be very useful to ISTPs who work in the field of economics, as securities analysts, or as market and sales analysts in business and industry—in short, in dealing with statistics in any field.

Some ISTPs, especially young ones, are great believers in economy of effort. This belief can contribute to their efficiency if they judge accurately how much effort is needed and proceed promptly to exert that much effort. However, if they underestimate or underperform, economy of effort can come perilously close to laziness, and little may get done.

Introverted Thinking Supported by Intuition

INTPs make scholars, theorists, and abstract thinkers in fields such as science, mathematics, economics, and philosophy. INTPs are perhaps the most intellectually profound of all the types. Intuition brings a deeper insight than is granted to thinking alone. It gives its possessors intellectual curiosity, quickness of understanding, ingenuity and fertility of ideas in dealing with problems, and an extra glimpse of possibilities that logic has not yet had time to reach. On the debit side, intuition makes routine harder, though an intuitive may, in the course of a lifetime, achieve a sufficient adaptation to it.

People of the INTP type, therefore, are particularly adapted to research and the attainment of new clarities. They are quite likely to be more interested in analyzing a problem and discovering where the solution lies than in carrying out their ideas. They formulate principles and create theories; they value facts only as evidence or as examples for a theory, never for their own sake.

A psychology professor of this type explained to an extraverted student, "This paper is perfectly correct, but you have put so much more stress on the facts than on the principle that it is obvious that you consider the facts the most important part. Therefore, your mark is a "B." The student was far more indignant over the reason than over the grade. "But *of course* the facts are the most important part," she said.

Many scholars of this type are teachers, especially on the university level, because the university values their attainments, and they themselves value the opportunity for study and research; but it is characteristic of their teaching that they care more for the subject than for the students. Gauss, the great mathematician, found teaching so painful that he tried to discourage all prospective students by telling them that the course about which they were inquiring would probably not be given at all.

The problem of communication also hampers their teaching. When confronted by a simple question that needs a simple answer, the introverted thinkers feel bound to state the exact truth, with every qualification that their scholarly consciences dictate; the answer is so exact and so complicated that few can follow it. If the teachers would scale down their explanation until it seemed, in their own opinion, too simple and obvious to be worth saying, they would have it just about right for general consumption.

INTP executives are probably rare outside scientific or academic circles. The good executives will be those who have acquired a very definite facility at extraversion sufficient to keep them in touch with the situations they must handle. Exercising their authority in a perceptive manner, such INTPs will use ingenuity and understanding to find ways of achieving the desired ends. But they will test every proposed measure by the exacting yardstick of their principles, so that whatever they direct will embody their own integrity.

The temptation for INTPs (as well as for extraverts with intuition) is to *assume* that an attractive possibility suggested by their intuition is as possible as it looks. They need to check out even their most attractive intuitive projects against the relevant facts and the limitations these facts impose. Otherwise they may find too late that they have squandered their energies in pursuit of an impossibility.

Extraverted Feeling Types
ESFJ and ENFJ

- Value, above all, harmonious human contacts

- Are best at jobs dealing with people and in situations where needed cooperation can be won by good will

- Are friendly, tactful, sympathetic, able almost always to express the feelings appropriate to the moment

- Are sensitive to praise and criticism, and anxious to conform to all legitimate expectations

- Possess outwardly directed judgment, which likes to have things decided and settled

- Are persevering, conscientious, orderly even in small matters, and inclined to insist that others be the same

- Are idealistic and loyal, capable of great devotion to a loved person or institution or cause

- May use thinking judgment occasionally to help in appreciating and adapting to points made by a thinker, but thinking is never permitted to oppose feeling aims

The extraverted feeling types radiate warmth and fellowship, and they have a vital need to find corresponding feelings in others and to meet a warm response. They are particularly warmed by approval and sensitive to indifference. Much of their pleasure and satisfaction comes not only from others' warm feelings but from their own; they enjoy admiring people and so tend to concentrate on a person's most admirable qualities.

They are remarkably able to see value in other people's opinions, and even when the opinions are conflicting, they have faith that harmony can somehow be achieved and often manage to bring it about.

Their intense concentration on other people's viewpoints sometimes makes them lose sight of the value of their own. They think best when talking with people and they enjoy talk.

All their mental processes seem to operate best by contact. Van der Hoop says, "Their thoughts take shape while being expressed" (1939, p. 84). However, thoughts arising through and during the process of expression often seem lengthy and clumsy to a rapid abstract thinker. There is probably an advantage for lecturers and orators in this blending of thought with speech, but it hinders extraverted feeling types from being brief and businesslike, and it often slows them down on the job. They tend to spend a great deal of time in conferences and committee meetings.

Their well-known idealism works two ways. They try hard to achieve their ideals, and they idealize those persons and institutions they prize. In both instances, extraverted feeling types are bound to repress and repudiate everything in themselves and in others that conflicts with feeling; this proceeding gives rise to a lack of realism wherever feeling is involved. (The extraverted sensing types resemble the extraverted feeling types in their ease and sociability; but when faced by the same cold, inharmonious fact, extraverted feeling denies its existence, and introverted feeling condemns its existence, whereas extraverted sensing accepts its existence and lets it go at that.)

Since the dominant process, feeling, is a judging process, these extraverted feeling types naturally prefer the judging attitude. It is not so much that they consciously enjoy settling things, as the extraverted thinkers usually do, but that they greatly like to have things settled, or at least to *feel* that things are settled. They tend to regard the world as a place where most of the decisions have already been made. The desirability or undesirability of most varieties of conduct, speech, opinion, and belief seems clear to them, a priori. They hold these truths to be self-evident. Thus, they are likely to have an immediate valuation of everything and an impulse to express it.

To have any validity, these judgments *must* be based on a well-developed perceptive process. If intuition is well developed as the auxiliary process, it will supply insight and understanding. If sensing is well developed as the auxiliary, it will supply first-hand, realistic knowledge of life. Either can furnish genuine grounds for feeling judgments, but if neither has been cultivated, there are no individual grounds to speak of.

Extraverted feeling types without a balancing auxiliary have, nonetheless, an urgent need to base their feeling judgments on *something*.

They have no recourse but to adopt the *forms* of feeling judgment that the community sanctions as suitable. Accordingly they adapt to the collective community, but their deficit of perception prevents them from adapting to other individuals.

One very unperceptive extraverted feeling type, who was having a great deal of trouble with her teen-age children, was persuaded to try to suspend judgment and consistently use the perceptive, unjudging attitude with them. She reported, "It works like a charm, but it's the hardest thing I ever did."

In the absence of adequate perception, the extraverted feeling types are prone to jump to conclusions and to act on assumptions that turn out to be wrong. They are especially likely to be blind to the facts when there is a disagreeable situation or painful criticism. It is harder for them than for other types to look squarely at things that they wish were not true; actually it is even hard for them to see such things at all. If they fail to face disagreeable facts, they will ignore their problems instead of finding good solutions.

Extraverted Feeling Supported by Sensing

ESFJs tend to be matter-of-fact and practical, conventional, copiously and factually conversational, and interested in possessions, beautiful homes, and all the tangible adornments of living. ESFJs are primarily concerned with the details of direct experience—their own, that of their friends and acquaintances, even the experience of strangers whose lives happen to touch theirs.

In a 1965 study by Harold Grant (see p. 157), ESFJs were the one type that chose "an opportunity to be of service to others" as the most important feature of the ideal job. They are more attracted to pediatrics than to any other medical specialty, and they are more strongly attracted to it than any other type. Their compassion and concern for physical conditions often take them into health professions, particularly nursing, where they provide warmth and comfort as well as devoted care. (Together with their counterpart, ISFJ, they had the lowest drop-out rate in my 1964 study of nursing students; see McCaulley, 1978.)

Even in office jobs their feeling plays a prominent role, and they manage to inject an element of sociability into any work they are assigned. Of all the types, they make the best adjustment to routine. They may not care too much what kind of work they do, but they want to be able to talk while they do it, and they want to work in a friendly atmosphere. A telephone company employee opposed a transfer to another unit, until she was assured that she would be given a farewell party by her old associates and a welcoming party by her new ones. Raised to the level of a social event, the change became acceptable to her feeling.

Extraverted Feeling Supported by Intuition

ENFJs tend to have curiosity for new ideas as such, taste for books and academic interests in general, tolerance for theory, vision and insight, and imagination for new possibilities beyond what is present or obvious or known. ENFJs are likely to have a gift of expression, but they may use it in speaking to audiences rather than in writing.

The NF combination of warmth and insight reaches its warmest and most gracious aspect in this type. ENFJs do well in many fields, for example, as teachers, clergy, career and personal counselors, and psychiatrists. Apparently the urge to harmonize extends even to intellectual opinions. A very charming ENFJ who has been interested in type since her high school days told me earnestly, "So-and-so asked me what I thought of type, and I didn't know what to tell her, because I didn't know how she felt about it."

Introverted Feeling Types
ISFP and INFP

- Value, above all, harmony in the inner life of feeling

- Are best at individual work involving personal values—in art, literature, science, psychology, or the perception of needs

- Have feelings that are deep but seldom expressed, because inner tenderness and passionate conviction are both masked by reserve and repose

- Maintain independence from the judgment of others, being bound by inner moral law

- Direct judgment inwardly toward keeping all lesser values subordinate to the greater

- Have a strong sense of duty and faithfulness to obligations, but no desire to impress or influence others

- Are idealistic and loyal, capable of great devotion to a loved person, purpose, or cause

- May use thinking judgment occasionally to help in winning a thinker's support of feeling aims, but is never permitted to oppose those aims

Introverted feeling types have a wealth of warmth and enthusiasm, but they may not show it until they know someone well. They wear their warm side inside, like a fur-lined coat. Reliance on feeling leads them to judge everything by personal values; they know what is most important to them, and they protect it at all costs.

As their feeling is introverted, they conduct their outer lives mainly with their preferred perceptive process, either sensing or intuition. This makes them open-minded, flexible, and adaptable—until one of the things they value most deeply seems in danger: Then they stop adapting.

They work twice as well at jobs they believe in; their feeling adds energy to their efforts. They want their work to contribute to something that matters to them—human understanding or happiness or health or perhaps the perfection of a project or undertaking. They want to have a purpose behind their paycheck, no matter how big the check. They are perfectionists whenever their feeling is engaged and are usually happiest at individual work.

The effectiveness of introverted feeling types depends on their finding a channel through which to give outward expression to their inner certainties and ideals. When this is possible, the inner certainties lend direction, power, and purpose to the introverted feeling types. Lacking such an outlet, the certainties make these people more sensitive and vulnerable when relationships fall short of their ideals. The result may be a sense of impotence and inferiority, with loss of confidence and distrust in life.

The contrast between the real and the ideal weighs more heavily upon the ISFPs, who are more sharply aware of the actual state of affairs, than upon the INFPs, whose intuition suggests hopeful avenues of improvement. The ISFPs are also more likely to suffer a consequent deficit of self-confidence. For both, the contrast offers a more acute problem than for the other types.

The solution comes with whole-hearted use of perception and understanding as a way of life. Because this is their destined mode of adaptation to the world, they must have proper faith in it, work at it, and be able to use it on both outer and inner difficulties. Relying on perception, they do not even try to bull their way through an obstacle; they "see" their way through. If they meet with distrust, indifference, or antagonism, which can block their outer endeavors or threaten their inner peace, they will often accomplish, by understanding, what could never be achieved by decisive frontal assault. Aesop told about a traveler who shed his cloak beneath the rays of the sun, after the wind's fiercest efforts had failed to tear it from him. Most people do thaw in the warmth of genuine, uncritical understanding.

The confidence of the introverted feeling types in their way of life should not be diminished at all because it does not *look* as masterful as that of the opposite types, those who depend on extraversion instead of introversion, or thinking instead of feeling, or judgment instead of perception, or even those who combine all three, like the extraverted thinkers who outwardly appear to be the most self-confident of all the types.

The introverted feeling types have their own masteries. They can accomplish certain things which others cannot, and the value of their contributions is second to none. Realization of the diverse excellences of the various types, whereby the difference between one type and another type is seen as a virtue rather than a defect, should strengthen their trust in their own gifts. It should also partially relieve the conflict that they are likely to feel when they cannot agree with those whom they love or admire.

Introverted Feeling Supported by Sensing

ISFPs see the realities—the needs of the moment—and try to meet them. ISFP is one of only two types, out of all sixteen, who strongly *prefer* general medical practice, which involves them with the widest variety of human ills. They may also find a satisfactory outlet in fields that value taste, discrimination, and a sense of beauty and proportion. They excel in craftsmanship. They seem to have a special love of nature and sympathy for animals. They are much less articulate than the INFPs, and the work of their hands is usually more eloquent than anything they say.

They may be particularly fitted for work that requires both devotion and a great adaptability, as is the case of visiting nurses, who can never count on standard conditions but must grasp each new situation and revise their instructions to fit the present circumstances.

They consistently tend to underestimate and understate them-selves. Probably ISFP is the most modest type. Anything ISFPs do well, they take for granted as no great achievement. They do not need St. Paul's injunction "not to think of themselves more highly than they ought to think." In most cases, they ought to think more highly than they do.

Introverted Feeling Supported by Intuition

INFPs excel in fields that deal with possibilities for people, such as counseling, teaching, literature, art, science, research, and psychology. The inclusion of science may be a surprise. It was to me. My father, Lyman J. Briggs, was director of the National Bureau of Standards, and we fully expected research scientists to be mainly INT like him, certainly not INF like my mother and myself. As it turned out, the INFs among the top researchers at the Bureau were indeed fewer than the INTs, but no less distinguished. Perhaps the enthusiasm generated by the feeling of an INF spurs intuition to reach a truth that analysis by thinking will confirm in due course.

INFPs usually have a gift for language. The high school senior class that was analyzed during the early validation of the Type Indicator included four INFP women. One was the editor of the school magazine and was voted by the class "most likely to succeed." One was editor of the yearbook, literary editor of the magazine, and valedictorian. The third was the winner of a four-year open scholarship and became the editor of her college paper. The fourth, who had the same combination of imagination and language but less ability to use it in the outer world, wrote haunting poetry in which she spoke for the "dreamers" who "drift across the horizons of the living."

The literary tendency evident in this type derives from the combi-nation of intuition and feeling. Intuition supplies imagination and insight, feeling supplies the urge to communicate and share, and the command of language is apparently a joint product of intuition's facility with symbols and feeling's artistic discrimination and taste. Thus, all four NF types should have the aptitude. However, the extravert types, ENFP and ENFJ, and even the introverted intuitives who extravert with feeling, INFJ, are likely to take a shortcut and do their communicating by the spoken word, as teachers, clergy, psychologists, and so on. Introverted feeling in INFPs is so reserved that they often prefer the *written* word as the way to communicate what they feel without making personal contact.

Extraverted Sensing Types
ESTP and ESFP

- Are realistic

- Are matter-of-fact and practical

- Are adaptable, usually easy-going, very much at home in the world, tolerant of others and of themselves

- Are endowed with a great capacity for enjoying life and a zest for experience of all kinds

- Are fond of concrete facts and good at details

- Are apt to learn most and best from experience, making a better showing in life than in school.

- Are usually conservative, valuing custom and convention, and liking things as they are

- Are able to absorb an immense number of facts, like them, remember them, and profit by them

The greatest strength of the extraverted sensing types is their realism. They primarily rely on the testimony of their own senses— what they see and hear and know firsthand—and thus are always aware of the actual situation around them. Types with feeling dominant are often prone to see things as they "should" be; types with thinking dominant to see things as they logically "must" be; types with intuition dominant to see things as they can be made to be; but the extraverted sensing types, as far as the eye can reach, see things as they are. An effortless economy characterizes their approach to a situation. They never fight the facts; instead, they accept and use them. They do not uselessly buck the line. If what they have started to do is blocked, they do it another way. They will follow no plan that has ceased to fit the circumstances.

Frequently they do just as well without a plan. They enjoy dealing with a situation as it arises; they are confident that a solution will always be revealed by a complete grasp of the facts. Unhampered by "should" or "must," they go after the facts and come up with an eminently practical solution.

As a result, people of this type may prove to be remarkably good at pulling conflicting factions together and making things run smoothly.

Their harmonizing ability owes much to their awareness of all the factual and personal elements in the situations that confront them. They can accept and deal with people as they are, and not be fooled about their quality.

Their enjoyment and absorption of facts is an essential function of a vigorous curiosity. One extraverted sensing type wrote to me, "It is true that I have in the back of my head a tremendous volume of facts on wholly unrelated subjects, and I am always interested in more." Like other ES types, the ESTPs and ESFPs are curious about anything new that is presented directly to their senses—new food, scenery, people, activities, objects, gadgets or contrivances. However, new things that cannot be grasped through the senses—abstract ideas, theories, and so on—seem less real and are much less acceptable: Anything mysterious is rather distasteful, as it undermines the security of a factual world. A new idea is never wholly liked or trusted until there has been time to master it and fix it firmly in a framework of solid fact.

Therefore extraverted sensing types are at their best in dealing with variations in the known and familiar rather than with what is entirely new. Their strong point is their flawless handling of things and situations, preferably spiced with some variety.

Often they have an instinctive affinity for machinery and a sure sense of what it can and cannot be made to do. Among the first twenty men whom we identified as extraverted sensing types, we found a top-notch mechanical engineer, a precision machinist, a very successful teacher of engineering shop, a Naval "crash officer," and a government expert whose detailed study of the tangled wreckage of crashed planes has led to the detection of obscure but fatal flaws in airplane design.

On the personal side, these types are strong in the art of living. They value material possessions and take the time to acquire, care for, and enjoy them. They greatly value concrete enjoyment, from good food and good clothes to music, art, the beauties of nature, and all the products of the amusement industry. Even without these aids, they get a lot of fun out of life, which makes them fun company. They enjoy physical exercise and sports, and they are usually good at these; if not, they are good rooters for those who are.

In school, they have no great regard for books as a preparation for life or as a substitute for first-hand experience. Most of their studying is memory work; although that technique suffices in some courses, it is not enough in physics and math, in which principles must be understood. There is a story about a general, notable throughout his career for his skillful handling of troops in the field, who nevertheless had nearly flunked out of West Point when he tried to pass a course in tactics by remembering the lectures word for word.

Van der Hoop says of these people, "They are most impressed by facts, and their originality finds expression in a truer and less prejudiced view of these than others take.... They fight somewhat shy of ideals. They stick to experience, are empiricists par excellence, and are in general conservative in their practical life, if they see no prospect of advantage in change. They are pleasant people, good comrades, and jolly boon companions... frequently good storytellers.... They often make good observers, and they make good practical use of their observations.... There is great capacity for perception of details and for practical evaluations based on them; further, there is the power to make sound estimations in regard to usefulness and serviceability" (1939, p. 927).

These types naturally prefer the perceptive attitude, so their virtues tend to be open-mindedness, tolerance, and adaptability, rather than sustained effort, methodology, and decisiveness. The latter qualities appear only with a superior development of judgment to balance the sensing. It is extremely important for these people to cultivate enough thinking judgment or feeling judgment to give them continuity, purpose, and character. Otherwise, there will be danger of laziness, instability, and a generally shallow personality.

Extraverted Sensing Supported by Thinking

ESTPs make decisions with thinking rather than feeling and therefore are more aware of the logical consequences of an act or decision. Thinking gives ESTPs a better grasp of underlying principles, helps with math and theory, and makes it easier for them to get tough when the situation calls for toughness.

In dealing with mechanical and other concrete problems, they are solid and practical and avoid complexity. In straightforward matters, their judgment is accurate and reliable.

They tend to prefer action to conversation. The more directly a matter can be translated into action, the clearer and more effective they become. When they do sit around, it is in an attitude of friendly readiness to do almost any pleasurable thing.

Extraverted Sensing Supported by Feeling

ESFPs make decisions with feeling rather than thinking. Feeling tends to center interest and observation on people, which gives rise to a marked friendliness, tact, and ease in handling human contacts, as well as a sound and practical estimate of people. Among ESFPs are the students whose high school class voted them "the friendliest" or "the best sport." Feeling also makes for artistic taste and judgment, but is no help with analysis. It may make this type too lenient as disciplinarians.

Introverted Sensing Types
ISTJ and ISFJ

- Are systematic, painstaking, and thorough

- Carry responsibility especially well, but ISTJ generally likes it better than ISFJ

- Are very hard working; they are the most practical of the introvert types

- Are outwardly matter-of-fact, inwardly entertained by extremely individual reactions to their sense impressions

- Are conspicuous for patient and willing application to detail

- Make an excellent adaptation to routine

- Absorb and enjoy using an immense number of facts

Introverted sensing types are made remarkably dependable by their combination of preferences. They use their favorite process, sensing, in their inner life, and they base their ideas on a deep, solid accumulation of stored impressions, which gives them some almost unshakable ideas. Then they use their preferred kind of judgment, thinking or feeling, to run their outer life. Thus, they have a complete, realistic, practical respect both for the facts and for whatever responsibilities these facts create. Sensing provides the facts, and after the introverts' characteristic pause for reflection, their judgment accepts the responsibilities.

They look on tempests and are never shaken. The interaction of introversion, sensing, and the judging attitude gives them extreme stability. They do not enter into things impulsively, but once in, they are very hard to distract, discourage, or stop (unless events convince them that they are wrong). They lend stability to everything with which they are connected.

Their use of experience contributes to their stability. They habitually compare present and past situations. Used in an executive capacity, this quality makes for consistent policy and for care in the introduction of changes. Used in evaluating people or methods, it can marshal numerous incidents to support a conclusion.

They like everything kept factual and stated clearly and simply. In van der Hoop's words, they "cannot take intuition seriously, and they regard its activity in others with misgiving" (1939, p. 33). They have "great capacity for perception of details and for practical evaluations based on them.... In their own field these people are usually very much at home, having a good mastery of the technical side of their calling, but without regarding this as any special merit. They accept both what they can and what they cannot do, as simple facts, but they tend on the whole to underestimate themselves" (1939, p. 32). Their success often comes by way of others who recognize and place a higher value on their good qualities and provide an environment in which they can be most productive.

Along with their solid and evident virtues, they have one odd and charming quality that may not be apparent until they are very well known. Their sense impressions cause a *vivid private reaction* to the essence of the thing sensed. The reaction is all their own and unpredictable. It is impossible to know what droll and unexpected associations of ideas take place behind their outer calm. Only when they are "off duty"— relaxing from extraversion, responsibility, and the judging attitude— will they sometimes give spontaneous expression to this inner perception. Then they *may* say what comes into their minds and give others a glimpse of their' perceptions and associations, which may be absurd, irreverent, touching, or hilarious, but never predictable, because their way of sensing life is intensely individual.[10]

When they are "on duty" and dealing with the world, the personality they show reflects the judging processes they habitually use outwardly, that is, their auxiliary, either thinking or feeling.

Introverted Sensing Supported by Thinking

ISTJs emphasize logic, analysis, and decisiveness. With enough extraversion, ISTJs make able executives. They also make exhaustively thorough lawyers who take nothing for granted and thus catch many slips and oversights that others make. All contracts should be cleared by ISTJs; they will overlook nothing that is in it and assume nothing that is not.

This is a fine type for accountants. It also appears to be ideal for dictating-machine transcribers. The head of a central transcription department selected three operators as having the perfect temperament for the work; they were chosen for their accuracy, continuity, concentration, and ability to be content without socializing at work. All three were well-marked ISTJ women, though apparently only about one woman in twenty-three belongs to this type.[11]

ISTJs will give any amount of help if they can see that it is needed, but their logic rebels against requirements or expectation to do anything that doesn't make sense to them. Usually they have difficulty understanding needs that differ widely from their own. But once they are convinced that something matters a great deal to a given person, the need becomes a fact worthy of respect; they may go to generous lengths to help satisfy it, although they still hold that it doesn't make sense. In fact, they may be sharply critical of the carelessness or lack of foresight by which some unfortunate has landed in trouble and, all the same, spend much time and energy to help.

Sometimes ISTJs carry their type development beyond their dominant and auxiliary processes and achieve a marked supplementary development of their third-best process, feeling, for use in human relationships, especially for appreciating their closest friends.

Introverted Sensing Supported by Feeling

ISFJs emphasize loyalty, consideration, and the common welfare. This is a fine type for a family doctor. The use of feeling in contacts with patients supplies the warmth and reassurance they crave, and the highly-cultivated sensing neglects no symptom and is able to draw on an accurate and encyclopedic memory.

This is also a fine type for the nurses. In a sample of students I gathered from nursing schools from coast to coast, ISFJ showed the highest self-selection into the profession and the lowest drop-out rate during training. The low drop-out rate testifies to their motivation and follow-through.

One outstanding member of the type is a two-star general. His well-balanced type gives him three qualities said to have been recommended by diverse military authorities: the shock-absorbing mental robustness, which is the first requirement for a general according to General Sir Archibald Wavell; the painstaking attention to administration and supply, which Socrates puts first on his list; and the strict realism of sensing, which Napoleon preferred to its intuitive opposite in his dictum, "There are men who, by their...make-up, create for themselves a complete picture built upon a single detail. Whatever...other good qualities they may have, nature has not marked them for the command of armies."

All three qualities are consistent with either thinking or feeling as auxiliary. The two-star general's judging process, strongly developed feeling, is masked in practice by deep reserve. The feeling is expressed as loyalty to duty and scrupulous concern for the interests of his subordinates, which evokes affection and loyalty in return.

The outstanding merits of the type are also found in dissimilar occupations. The most careful worker I ever encountered, a floor-finisher in business for himself, showed the typical qualities. He was assisted by his son, an easy-going young extravert, who testified with rueful admiration that "the old man is particular as hell."

Both ISTJ and ISFJ, of course, need to be balanced by a substantial development of either thinking or feeling. Judgment helps them deal with the world; it balances the introverted perception, which by itself is not interested in the outside world. If judgment is not developed, they largely ignore the outside world and become uncommunicative and incomprehensible, absorbed in subjective reactions to sensory impressions and lacking outlets for their qualities.

Well-balanced types have both judgment and perception well developed. Their problem is to use the right one at the right time. Like all the other judging types, ISTJ and ISFJ are more prone to use the judging attitude when perception would be more appropriate than to make the opposite mistake. Hence the question is: When should a judging type not use judgment? And the answer is: When dealing with other people.

Regardless of type, the proper use of judgment is on one's own actions and problems. For use on other people, perception is fairer, kinder, and more productive.

Extraverted Intuitive Types
ENTP and ENFP

- Are alert to all the possibilities

- Are original, individual, independent, but also extremely perceptive of the views of others

- Are strong in initiative and creative impulse, but not so strong in completing projects

- Have lives that are likely to be a succession of projects

- Are stimulated by difficulties and most ingenious in solving them

- Operate by impulsive energy rather than concentrated will-power

- Are tireless at what interests them, but find it hard to get other things done

- Hate routine

- Value inspiration above everything else and follow it confidently into all manner of opportunities, enterprises, ventures and adventures, explorations, researches, mechanical inventions, promotions and projects

- Are versatile, often startlingly clever, enthusiastic, easy with people, and full of ideas about everything under the sun

- At their best, are gifted with insight amounting to wisdom and with the power to inspire

Extraverted intuitives are hard to describe because of their infinite variety. Their interest, enthusiasm, and energy pour suddenly into unforeseeable channels like a flash flood, sweeping everything along, overwhelming all obstacles, carving out a path which others will follow long after the force that made it has flowed on into other things.

The force that animates extraverted intuitives is not conscious willpower or even a planned purpose, as in the case of the judging types. It is a perceptive energy—an intuitive vision of some possibility in the external world, which they feel to be peculiarly their own because they "saw it first" in a very original and personal way. Aside from any practical consideration, they feel charged with a mission to realize that possibility. The possibility has an irresistible pull, an undeniable claim upon them. It becomes their master and in its service they may forget to eat or sleep. They cannot rest until they get the genie out of the bottle. As Jung says, "Emerging possibilities are compelling motives from which intuition cannot escape, and to which all else must be sacrificed" (1923, p. 464). However, once they get the genie out or even reach the point where everyone recognizes that it *can* be got out, it does not interest them anymore. The genie is no longer a possibility; it is a mere fact. Somebody else can take over from there.

To call this loss of interest fickle, as the judging types are apt to do, is to miss the point. The intuitives have an essential duty to perform in the world: They have to see to it that human inspirations are not wasted. They cannot tell in advance whether an inspiration is going to work out; they have to throw themselves into it, heart and soul—and see. When they have seen, they have to go on to new possibilities, armed with all they have learned from the old. The intuitives are as stubbornly loyal to their guiding principle, the inspiring possibility, as the sensing types are to the facts, or the feeling types to their hierarchy of values, or the thinkers to their thought out conclusions.

Thus intuitives' lives tend to be a series of projects. If they are lucky enough to find their calling in a line of work that permits such a stream of projects, the successive enthusiasms build themselves into a coherent career. For writers, it may be a sequence of books, each presenting a different problem to be solved, written, and put on the shelf. For a person in business, it may be successive expansions of the business into new fields; for a salesperson, the conquest of new prospects; for a politician, a progression of campaigns for higher and higher offices; for a college professor, the renewed challenge of an entering class; and for a psychiatrist, the intricate mystery of each new patient's mind.

If the intuitives' pursuit of authentic inspirations is completely blocked, they will feel imprisoned, bored, and desperately discontent. These are external difficulties to which they are not likely to submit for long. Intuition will almost always find a way out.

There are, however, two *internal* dangers that are more serious. First, intuitives must not squander their energies. In a world full of possible projects, they must pick those that have potential value, either intrinsically or for the intuitives' own development. Then, having started, they must not quit. They must persevere until they have established something—that the idea works or does not work, that they should or should not go on. It is not quitting if an intuitive woman writes one good mystery and stops because mystery writing is not what she wants to do the rest of her life; but it *is* quitting if she stops in the middle or finishes badly what she could finish well.

On both these counts, the choosing and the perseverance, intuitives need the stabilizing influence of well-developed thinking or feeling. Either can give them a standard for evaluating their inspirations and provide them with the strength of character and self-discipline for persevering through the duller stretches of work.

Intuitives without judgment do not finish things (this is particularly conspicuous because they start so many), are not stimulated by obstacles as the well-balanced intuitives are, and are unstable, undependable, easily discouraged, and, as many of them freely admit, do not do anything that they do not want to do.

Extraverted intuitives must, therefore, begin to develop their judgment as early as possible. The type can usually be recognized at a very early age. Van der Hoop notes that "children of this type are merry and full of the joy of life; but often extremely tiring. They are always thinking out something fresh, and their imagination continually suggests fresh possibilities. They have a finger in every pie, want to know every-thing...and at an early age want to be something special" (1939, p. 43). For example, they take far less interest in meeting basic school requirements than in doing something extra or out of the ordinary. For their own welfare, the spectacular and unexpected should not be accepted *in lieu of* the fundamentals.

Disciplining them is not easy, because they enjoy from the cradle a remarkable ability to get what they want from people. This gift is a combination of ingenuity, charm, and understanding the other person. It lets them proceed with great confidence. I once suggested to a three-year-old that his mother would probably spank him for what he was doing. "No," he said serenely. "My mother doesn't know the right things."

In later life, that uncanny faculty of appraisal produces the teachers who can divine the unguessed potentials of a student, the psychologists who can accurately estimate an IQ on the basis of a brief interview, and the executives whose genius lies in their selection and use of subordinates.

Combined with compelling enthusiasm for their goals, this understanding of people may render the extraverted intuitives very effective leaders, able to persuade others of the worth of their own vision and to rally their support and cooperation.

Extraverted Intuition Supported by Thinking

ENTPs are somewhat more likely than ENFPs to take an executive direction. ENTPs tend to be independent, analytical, and impersonal in their relations with people, and they are more apt to consider how others may affect their projects than how their projects may affect others. They may be inventors, scientists, trouble-shooters, promoters, or almost anything that it interests them to be.

Extraverted Intuition Supported by Feeling

ENFPs are more enthusiastic than ENTPs and more concerned with people and skillful in handling them. ENFPs are drawn to counseling, where each new person presents a fresh problem to be solved and fresh possibilities to be communicated. They may be inspiring teachers, scientists, artists, advertising or salespeople, or almost anything they want to be.

Introverted IntuitiveTypes
INTJ and INFJ

- Are driven by their inner vision of the possibilities

- Are determined to the point of stubbornness

- Are intensely individualistic, though this shows less in INFJs, who take more pains to harmonize their individualism with their environment

- Are stimulated by difficulties, and most ingenious in solving them

- Are willing to concede that the impossible takes a little longer—but not much

- Are more interested in pioneering a new road than in anything to be found along the beaten path

- Are motivated by inspiration, which they value above everything else and use confidently for their best achievements in any field they choose—science, engineering, invention, political or industrial empire-building, social reform, teaching, writing, psychology, philosophy, or religion

- Are deeply discontented in a routine job that offers no scope for inspiration

- Are gifted, at their best, with a fine insight into the deeper meanings of things and with a great deal of drive

As with all introverts, the outward personality of introverted intuitives is strongly influenced by their auxiliary process. For example, two of the most outstanding officer candidates in a Naval training unit were both introverted intuitives. The one whose auxiliary process was thinking (INTJ) was appointed battalion commander for three successive terms and made a crisp, efficient executive. The one whose auxiliary process was feeling (INFJ) was *elected* to the three highest offices the student body could bestow: president of student government, chairman of the executive committee, and president of his class. A woman who knew them both well summed up the contrast by saying that if both were aboard a ship that was torpedoed, the INTJ would be primarily interested in controlling the damage, but the INFJ's primary concern would be the crew's welfare. They agreed that she was right.

Among research scientists and design engineers, introverted intuitives stand at the top. INTJs are somewhat more likely than INFJs to be interested in scientific and technical matters, but when INFJs are interested, they appear to be just as good. In an academic setting, INFJs may be even better, probably because feeling is more eager to meet a teacher's demands, whereas thinking is likely to criticize the way a course is conducted and refuse to bother with items it considers irrelevant.

Thinking or feeling judgment is vitally necessary, and introverted intuitives must develop it for themselves, because their utter conviction of their intuition's validity makes them impervious to the influence of outside judgment. The importance to introverted intuitives of cultivating a judging process to balance and support their intuition cannot be overemphasized .

Their greatest gifts come directly from their intuition—the flashes of inspiration, the insight into relationships of ideas and meaning of symbols, the imagination, the originality, the access to resources of the unconscious, the ingenuity, and the visions of what could be. These are all inner gifts on the perceptive side. Without a developed auxiliary judging process, they will have little or no development of an outer personality and equally limited use of the gifts. However, a good judging process in support will shape the intuitive perceptions into conclusions or actions that will have a sound impact on the outer world.

Van der Hoop recognized this problem:

> There is peculiar difficulty, where this inner knowledge is concerned, in finding even approximate expression for what is perceived. It is extremely important, therefore, for people of this type to attain through their education a technique of expression....

The development of this type is slower and more arduous than that of most other people.... Such children are not very amenable to influence from their environment. They may have periods of uncertainty and reserve, after which they suddenly become very determined, and if then they are opposed, they may manifest an astonishing self-will and obstinacy. As a result of the intensely spontaneous activity within, they are frequently moody, occasionally brilliant and original, then again reserved, stubborn and arrogant.

In later life, also, it is a persistent characteristic of people of this type, that while on the one hand they possess great determination, on the other hand they find it very difficult to express what they want. Although they may have only a vague feeling about the way they want to go, and of the meaning of their life, they will nevertheless reject with great stubbornness anything that does not fit in with this. They fear lest external influences or circumstances should drive them in a wrong direction, and they resist on principle. (1939, p. 48)

It follows that these people cannot be successfully coerced. They will not even be *told* anything without their permission, but they will accept an offer of facts, opinions, or theories, for free consideration; the excellence of their understanding must be trusted to recognize what is true.

Introverted Intuition Supported by Thinking

INTJs are the most independent of all the sixteen types and take more or less conscious pride in that independence.

Whatever their field, they are likely to be innovators. In business, they are born reorganizers. Intuition gives them an iconoclastic imagination and an unhampered view of the possibilities; extraverted thinking supplies a keenly critical organizing faculty. "Whatever is, could doubtless be improved!" They are likely, however, to organize themselves out of a job. They cannot continually reorganize the same thing, and a finished product has no more interest. Thus, they need successive new assignments, with bigger and better problems, to stretch their powers.

With technical interests, they tend to be research scientists, inventors, and design engineers. They are likely to be very good at mathematics, especially problems, but not quite as adept at pure mathematical theory as INTPs. INTJs are fine at thinking things up, and definitely better at working things out than the INTPs. They can get things done, but they will be interested only when the problems involved are complicated enough to be challenging. Routine production would waste the intuition, and a purely theoretical research job would waste the extraverted thinking, which has a craving for practical applications of ideas.

Even when well-balanced, they have a tendency to ignore the views and feelings of other people. Use of the critical attitude in personal relations is a destructive luxury that can have a disintegrating effect upon their private lives. They would do well to make an effort to use their critical faculty on their impersonal problems and on themselves and to work for some development of appreciation (they need not call it feeling) to use on others.

Introverted Intuition Supported by Feeling

INFJs naturally concern themselves with people, sometimes so much as to appear extraverted. It is actually the feeling process, not the individual, that is extraverted, although the very evident fellowship and harmony may appear to be the basis of their personalities.

The individualism of the INFJs is often less conspicuous, not because their inner vision is less clear and compelling, but because they care enough about harmony to try to win (rather than demand) acceptance of their purposes. By the time they have induced others to understand, approve, and cooperate toward a goal, they have fitted both the goal and themselves quite naturally into the community pattern.

They may also seem, especially to themselves, less original than the INTJs. When intuition is focused on people and their problems, it does not have as much opportunity to dwell on the unforeseen as scientific intuition does. A masterpiece of insight into human relations may not look original at all. It is so accurate that it looks obvious.

The visions of the INFJs tend to concern human welfare, and their contributions are likely to be made independent of a mass movement. Occasionally, the individual contribution *starts* a mass movement or a religion or a crusade.

PART III

Practical
Implications of Type

CHAPTER 10

Use of the Opposites

EXCEPT IN AMAZINGLY objective readers, the foregoing type descriptions will have aroused more sympathy and approval for some types than for others. Each reader's type and those close to it can be expected to seem desirable and comfortable because they look at or value things in the ways that seem natural. Types that are quite different, reflecting different strengths and values, may not seem as desirable.

When good will is in short supply, the conflict of the opposites can be serious. Type theory is informally confirmed by the difficulty that opposite types have in getting along with each other, and the saving of friction that often results when they understand the basis of their opposition.

Disagreement suddenly becomes less irritating when Smith recognizes that it would hardly be normal for Jones to agree. Jones starts from a different point of view and proceeds in a different direction. So when Jones arrives at a conclusion far removed from Smith's own, it is not from being willfully contrary, but from simply being a different type.

In making such allowances, Smith needs to keep one hard fact in mind. Jones is not merely weak where Smith is strong: Jones is also strong where Smith is weak. Thinkers, for instance, notice the lack of logic in a feeling type, and they tend to underrate the other's judgment because it is not logical. They have reason to distrust feeling. Knowing their own feeling is erratic and not very serviceable, thinkers try to keep it out of their decisions and assume that other people's feeling is no more trustworthy than their own. Actually, the feeling of the feeling types is a more skilled kind of judge even than the thinker's thinking, for example, in judging which things people value most.

Similarly, intuitives notice that a sensing person does not handle ideas intuitively and are, therefore, likely to underrate the other's perception. They do not realize that the sensing person's awareness of realities is much keener than their own. Sensing people make an analogous mistake; relying on their superior grasp of realities, they are inclined to distrust all intuitive inspirations, because their own undeveloped intuition does not bring them much of value.

Ideally, such opposites should supplement each other in any joint undertaking, whether in business or marriage. An opposite approach to a problem is very likely to expose what has been overlooked. Too much oppositeness, however, can make working together difficult, even when people understand their difference of type. The best co-workers probably are people who differ on perception *or* judgment (but not both) and are alike on at least one other preference. This much difference is useful, and the two or three preferences they have in common help them to understand each other and communicate.

When two people reach a deadlock over the handling of a given situation, the trouble may be a result of their difference in type, which has interfered with their communication. When two people have not known the same facts, or not considered the same possibilities, or not foreseen the same consequences, each has only an incomplete knowledge of the problem. They must put it all together. Each needs to use all four processes, however well or ill developed: sensing to gather the relevant facts, intuition to see all measures that might usefully be taken, thinking to determine the consequences, and feeling to consider the impact of these consequences on the people involved. The pooling of their respective perceptions and judgments offers the best chance of finding a solution valid for them both.

The difficulties for any type are likely to lie in the fields belonging to that type's least skilled processes. For example, the types differ in their capacity for the analysis required to formulate a long-term policy in a complicated matter. Analyzing demands recognition of the basic principles involved, so that all the consequences of a proposed action may be foreseen, including those not intended or desired. Thus, analysis comes more easily to a thinking type than to a feeling type, and most easily when the thinking is the dominant and most-developed process. Thinking dissects a proposal with emphasis upon cause and effect, including all the foreseeable effects, whether pleasant or unpleasant. Feeling tends to concentrate on the value of one effect and to resist considering the drawbacks.

Analysis also comes more easily to introverts than to extraverts. Introverts can best deal with a situation by considering it an example of a reliable general principle; they are skilled in recognizing underlying principles. Extraverts deal with more situations, faster and somewhat more casually, and with less time out for reflection. They are faster, in part because they already know more of the circumstances. Information has a pleasant, useful way of rubbing off on them as they go about their daily business. Introverts can broaden the base for their analysis by finding out what extraverts can tell them about any situation.

For people who are neither thinkers nor introverts, the next best tool for analysis is intuition, a powerful instrument for discovering possibilities and relationships. It is quick and may yield brilliant results. However, strong NF types are likely to be short on realism; they should check their projects with a good ST to discover what facts and consequences they have overlooked.

Extraverts with neither thinking nor intuition, the ESF types, are likely to find analysis difficult. They deal much better with concrete and familiar problems, which can be handled face to face and on the basis of firsthand knowledge and personal experience. They should recognize their tendency to decide matters with an eye to the immediate situation and other people's wishes. By submitting a new proposal to a thinker, they can find out what is wrong with it in the long run—what principles or policies it violates; what precedents it establishes; what unexpected consequences may ensue; in short, what will be the cost of choosing the course that looks most pleasant at the moment. They will probably not like what the thinker tells them, but they should take it seriously.

Deciding on policy, however, is only part of the task. Often people need to sell their ideas to superiors, associates, and subordinates. Persuasion, a part of communication, comes most easily to the extraverts and the feeling types. Extraverts tend to express themselves freely, so their associates will be informed just by listening. The introverts' associates, who are much more in the dark on these points than the introverts realize, cannot be persuaded until ideas are communicated.

The feeling types tend to express themselves tactfully. Because they want harmony, they consider in advance what the impact on the other person will be and design their presentation for the specific listener. Accordingly, their proposals tend to get a more favorable hearing than do those of the thinkers. Unless thinkers carry their respect for cause and effect into the field of human relations, they may not have much awareness of people. As they set forth their own views, calmly and dispassionately but without reference to anyone else's, they often encounter surprising opposition.

No one, of course, can appreciate another's viewpoint unless it is understood. Perceptive types are more likely to understand it than judging types because they are more inclined to stop and listen.

No type has everything. The introverts and thinkers, though likely to arrive at the most profound decisions, may have the most difficulty in getting their conclusions accepted. The opposite types are best at communicating, but not as adept at determining the truths to be communicated.

For maximum effectiveness, all types must add to their natural endowment the appropriate use of the opposites, either by using them in other people or by developing a controlled use of them within them-selves. Examples of the former are highlighted in Figure 32. The latter is the crowning stage in type development. By the time individuals have full control of their dominant and auxiliary processes, they know their strengths and use them expertly. If they can then learn to use an opposite when it is more appropriate than the best-developed processes, they can become adequately skilled in its use and, when needed, can cross over from the natural to the appropriate. Crossing over is difficult but more easily achieved with an understanding of *why* the natural and automatic response is not necessarily the best.

For example, the thinker's natural process is inappropriate when used in personal relations with feeling types, because it includes a readiness to criticize. Criticism is of great value when thinkers apply it to their own conduct or conclusions, but it has a destructive effect upon feeling types, who need a harmonious climate.

The feeling types have a great need for sympathy and appreciation. They want others to realize how they feel and either share the feeling or at least acknowledge its value. They want others to approve of them and what they prize. They draw warmth and life from friendliness and get a painful and often crippling chill from antagonism. They hate to feel divided, even temporarily, from people whom they value.

Uninhibited criticism makes life stressful for feeling types. Ironi-cally, every defense against it makes it worse. Justification, argument, and counterattack only lead to further antagonism. Because peace and amity are their objectives, the feeling types have lost from the start. Some are defensive only occasionally and usually tolerate criticism in silence. Others try to defend themselves or to argue against the thinker. Either way, the damage is done.

People who are conscious of such damage and want to avoid it can improve matters. Feeling types can try to avoid taking criticism so

Figure 32. Mutual Usefulness of Opposite Types

Intuitive Types **Need SensingTypes**	**Sensing Types** **Need Intuitive Types**
To bring up pertinent facts	To bring up new possibilities
To apply experience to problems	To supply ingenuity on problems
To read the fine print in a contract	To read the signs of coming change
To notice what needs attention now	To see how to prepare for the future
To have patience	To have enthusiasm
To keep track of essential details	To watch for new essentials
To face difficulties with realism	To tackle difficulties with zest
To remind them that the joys of the present are important	To show that the joys of the future are worth looking for

Feeling Types **Need Thinking Types**	**Thinking Types** **Need Feeling Types**
To analyze	To persuade
To organize	To conciliate
To find the flaws in advance	To forecast how others will feel
To reform what needs reforming	To arouse enthusiasm
To hold consistently to a policy	To teach
To weigh "the law and the evidence"	To sell
To fire people when necessary	To advertise
To stand firm against opposition	To appreciate the thinker

personally; often it is not intended as an attack but is merely a form of self-expression.

Thinkers can do three things to limit the damage their criticism may cause. First, they can refrain from critical comment when they know it will do no good. Second, they can be careful not to exaggerate the faults they want changed. This is more important than it may seem. Extraverted thinkers tend to exaggerate for the sake of emphasis, and the victim will be too outraged by the unfair overstatement to pay attention to the part that is true. Third, they can remember how feeling types respond to sympathy and appreciation; a little of either will greatly tone down a necessary criticism, but the thinker must express the sympathy or appreciation first.

The third technique is effective both at home and at work. There is a crucial difference between "I think you're all wrong about Jones" and "I see why you feel that way, but I think you're probably wrong about Jones"; or between "Of course Bates lost the position. He should never have..." and "Tough on Bates to lose the position. He should never have..."

Usually a thinker does, to some extent, understand another's feelings and does think it is tough on Bates to lose the position, even though Bates brought it on himself. Those mitigating circumstances could just as well be mentioned if the thinker thought it worth the trouble. From the standpoint of human relations it is worth vastly more than the trouble it takes. The little sympathy or appreciation, coming first, puts the thinkers in the same camp with the feeling types, and the feeling types' desire to stay in the same camp will keep them agreeing with the thinkers as far as possible.

This technique improves with practice. In time it becomes automatic. The thinkers need only make an effort to mention the points on which they honestly agree or approve before proceeding to the points of difference. They will be astonished at how infrequently people will fight them on the points of difference, and their own neglected feeling side will be satisfied too.

An appropriate and brief crossover by the thinker to the use of the opposite process, feeling, can be tolerated by thinking because the feeling process is being used in the service of thinking; feeling helps win acceptance of the thinker's ideas and purposes. There is no abdication of authority, only a slight delegation.

The corresponding achievement for a feeling type is a brief crossover to the use of thinking in the service of feeling, for example, to outline in logical form the ideas and purposes determined by feeling judgment, to buttress them by logical arguments for a thinker's approval, or to foresee criticism that would be leveled at some cherished piece of work and correct the faults. When criticism is incurred despite efforts to disarm it, the feeling type might even use thinking to analyze and learn from the criticism.

However logical they may try to be, feeling types are never logical enough to estimate the full cost of something that appeals to them. They will benefit from consulting a genuine thinker and hearing the worst. The thinker should genuinely consider the merits of the proposal, and both can proceed with mutual profit.

The feeling type should be brief, however. The characteristic that probably annoys the thinkers most is the tendency of the feeling types to talk too much, with too many irrelevancies, and with too much detail and repetition. When there is something to be said, thinkers want it said concisely. The extraverted feeling types, as the father of one of them said, tend to have no "terminal facilities."

Sensing types and intuitives are another example of mutually useful opposites. The sensing person has faith in the actual, the intuitive in the possible. As each concentrates accordingly, they seldom look at anything from the same angle. The difference in viewpoint becomes acute, often exasperating, when the person with sensing has authority over the intuitive and the intuitive comes up with a blazing idea. The intuitive tends to present the idea in rough form—suitable for another intuitive—and expects the sensing listener to concentrate on the main point and ignore the sketchy details. The sensing person's natural reaction is to concentrate on what is missing, decide that the idea cannot work (and of course it cannot in that form), and flatly turn it down. One idea is wasted, one intuitive is frustrated, and one sensing executive has to deal with a resentful subordinate.

The collision could be avoided if either showed respect for the opposite process. The intuitive should be realistic enough to know what the executive's reaction will be and prepare for it, work out the details of the proposal, and organize the necessary facts in irrefutable form. Then, acknowledging the sensing types' appreciation of logical order, the intuitive should begin by emphasizing what problems the new idea will solve. (When dealing with an *intuitive* executive, a worker should avoid encouraging the executive to think about the problem lest the proposed solution be forestalled by new offhand suggestions.)

The sensing type should give the intuitive's idea a fighting chance, although not necessarily agree that it might work. The sensing executive can say, "It might work *if…*" and then bring up all the objections that experience suggests and ask, "What would you do about these?" The intuitive, happily concentrating on the obstacles (instead of unhappily concentrating on the executive), often creates a valuable solution, although in so doing the intuitive may revise the original idea beyond recognition.

Not only can the clash of personalities be averted, but a positive gain results from requiring the intuitive's project to be evaluated by the realism of the sensing type. If intuitives learn to acquire some of that realism for themselves, they can use their own sensing to examine the facts and increase their own effectiveness. Intuitives can tolerate crossovers that serve the intuitive's projects.

The corresponding achievement for sensing types is a crossover to the use of intuition for a look at future objectives and possibilities. They can justify this uncharacteristic daydreaming on the grounds that someday a wild-eyed intuitive will try to change everything, and they, as practical people, should be prepared to steer events in a sensible direction.

Although crossovers are very useful, the clearest vision of the future comes only from an intuitive, the most realistic practicality only from a sensing type, the most incisive analysis only from a thinker, and the most skillful handling of people only from a feeling type.

CHAPTER 11

Type and Marriage

DIFFERENCES IN TYPE between husband and wife may give rise to friction, but this can be diminished or eliminated when its origin is understood. Nothing in this chapter is intended to discourage anyone from marrying a person of largely opposite type, but such a marriage should be undertaken with full recognition that the other person is different and has a right to remain different, and with full willingness to concentrate on the virtues of the other's type rather than the defects.

The role of type in courtship and marital choice is subject to some debate. Proverbially, birds of a feather flock together. It seems only reasonable that the greater mutual understanding between couples with more likeness than difference should lead, on the whole, to greater mutual attraction and esteem. Among 375 married couples whose Indicators were obtained in the 1940s, the most frequent situation was for the couple to be alike on three of their four preferences rather than on only two, as would be expected by chance.[12]

On the other hand, Jung said of extraverts and introverts, "Sad though it is, the two types are inclined to speak very badly of one another...often come into conflict. This does not, however, prevent most men from marrying women of the opposite type" (1971, p. 517). Plattner (1950), a Swiss marriage counselor, wrote that in most marriages, extraverts marry introverts, and two Jungian analysts, Gray and Wheelwright (1944), advanced a theory of "complementary mating. "

The apparent conflict of evidence here is itself informative. The observers just cited were testifying about the marriages they saw in their own practices. Their clients were in marital or psychological difficulty or both. Jung is reported to have commented, "Of course, we analysts have to deal a lot with marriages, particularly those that go wrong because the types are too different sometimes and they don't understand each other at all." If the marriages seen by analysts have gone wrong because the types are too different, then analysts and marriage counselors would be expected to encounter more oppositeness than occurs in successful marriages, which may confirm the thesis that having two or three preferences in common contributes to the success of a marriage and lessens the need for counseling.

Among our 375 couples, there was significantly more similarity than difference between husband and wife on each of the four preferences. The most frequent similarity was on SN, which suggests that *seeing things the same way*, whether by sensing or by intuition, does more to make a man and woman understandable to each other than a shared preference on EI or TF or JP.

The percent distribution of the couples was as follows:

Alike on all preferences	9
Alike on three	35
Alike on two	33
Alike on one	19
Alike on none	4

Couples who were mainly alike outnumbered those who were mainly opposite by two to one. Among the couples who were alike on all preferences, most were feeling types and may have had harmony as a conscious goal in choosing a spouse. Among the couples who were different on all preferences, nearly all the husbands were thinkers.

The amount of likeness that two people actually find in a marriage may fall far short of what they expected. In this respect the extraverted male before marriage has a decided advantage over his introverted brother. He is more aware of what people are like, he circulates more, and he knows more women. He has a wider circle from which to choose and may have a somewhat clearer idea of what he is choosing. This wider and more informed choice may explain why 53 percent of the extravert husbands (but only 39 percent of the introverts) had at least three preferences in common with their wives.

The effect of a preference on marital choice seems to vary from type to type. The men who apparently cared most about likeness on EI were the FJ types with extraverted feeling. FJ types are supposed to be the most sympathetic and the most concerned with harmony. The FJ suitor may therefore be more sensitive to whether a partner shares the same preferences for amusements, use of leisure time, and amount of sociability. Such a person may consciously intend to marry someone with almost identical interests. In the study conducted in the 1940s, where the husband was FJ, he and his wife were alike on EI in 65 percent of the cases, compared with 51 percent for all other types combined.

The men most inclined to marry their opposites on EI were the introverts with thinking. They probably did so more from shyness than from any other reason. Perhaps for every thinking introvert male who knowingly selects a quiet, introvert female, there is another who unknowingly is selected by an outgoing extravert woman. Her sociability bridges over the awkwardness that usually bedevils his type at the start of a new friendship.

Regardless of who is the extravert and who is the introvert in a marriage, the differences in the sociability may cause problems. The extravert's wish for active sociability runs counter to the introvert's wish for privacy, especially when the introvert's work is socially demanding. The day's work may use up all the extraversion available; home represents a chance for the peace and quiet needed to regain a balance. If the extravert spouse wants to go out, to have people in, or at least to spend the time at home in conversation, frustration may develop. For the introvert, silence, some chance to think quietly, is essential and requires the partner's cooperation. This need is hard to explain and impossible for the extravert to understand unless it is explained. Once partners understand each other's needs for quiet or sociability, they can usually make constructive adjustments.

Likeness on TF should be hardest to achieve because there are more feeling women than thinking women in our culture, and more thinking men than feeling men, though these differences may be decreasing. In this 1940s sample, there were not enough feeling men for all the feeling women, nor enough thinking women for all the thinking men. At the very most, only 78 percent of the couples *could* be matched on TF.

Nevertheless, where the man was an extravert, 62 percent of the couples were alike on TF; where he was an introvert, 49 percent were alike. Where husband and wife were both extraverts, the similarity on TF rose to 66 percent, which is high considering that the maximum possible was only 78 percent.

It may be that extraverts find out sooner than the introverts about the effects of difference on TF. Extraverts are notably outspoken: If a thinker's outspoken criticisms hurt the feelings of a feeling type, and the feeling type's outspoken airing of those hurt feelings annoys the thinker, they can break up and try alternative relationships.

Likeness on JP seems to matter mainly to three extravert types: 65 percent of the ENTP and ENFP husbands (who live by spontaneity) married perceptive wives; 93 percent of the ESTJ husbands (who live by system, organization, and decisiveness) married judging wives. Of the rest of the couples, only 52 percent were alike on JP. There are practical advantages in having both judgment and perception represented in a marriage. Many decisions can comfortably be left to the partner who enjoys making them.

Likeness on SN is important to all types. The highest rate of likeness, 71 percent, occurred in couples where the wife preferred thinking to feeling. Evidently, a person who puts trust in logic prefers a spouse with a similar orientation.

On the whole, extravert men with their wider acquaintance achieve more similarity in their marriages than introverts do. Their percentage of likeness ranges from 58 percent to 66 percent on the four preferences. Except for a 62 percent on SN, the percentage of likeness for introvert men ranges only from 49 percent to 52 percent.

The conclusions that can be drawn from study of these 375 married couples are necessarily tentative. The subjects were mostly college graduates or parents of college students. They were volunteers, their ages ranging from 17 to 85. Most of the marriages took place between 1910 and 1950, and all the subjects but a few of the youngest took the Type Indicator after marriage.

From the study of this sample, several conclusions emerge. In these marriages, which were in no apparent difficulty, there is significantly more similarity than difference between husband and wife on each of the four preferences. This finding contrasts sharply with the observations of psychiatrists and marriage counselors that the marriages they see exhibit more type differences than similarities. Similarity would appear to contribute to the success of a marriage.

Preferences held in common simplify human relations. They furnish a shortcut to understanding people, because it is easier to understand likeness than to understand difference. When people understand and admire someone whose type is close to theirs, they are, in a way, appreciating their own best qualities, which is enjoyable and productive though perhaps not as educational as appreciating someone quite different.

Even with only a single preference in common, a marriage can be wonderfully good (as I can testify) if the man and woman take the necessary pains to understand, appreciate, and respect each other. They will not regard differences between them as signs of inferiority, but as interesting variations in human nature, which enrich their lives. As one young ISTJ husband said of his ENFP wife, "If she were just like me, it wouldn't be any fun!"

Understanding, appreciation, and respect make a lifelong marriage possible and good. Similarity of type is not important, except as it leads to these three. Without them, people fall in love and out of love again; with them, a man and a woman will become increasingly valuable to each other and know that they are contributing to each other's lives. They consciously value each other more and know they are valued in return. Each walks taller in the world than would be thinkable alone.

Of course there are problems along the way, for example, the partner's faults. Those faults are probably only the reverse side of the partner's most admirable traits. A feeling man may value very much his thinking wife's strength, presence of mind in crisis, steadiness in the face of possible disaster. The thinker is not going to take small things very seriously, except to note what should be done or should have been done. A thinker may fall in love with a feeling type's warm, quick response, which nourishes the thinker's own half-starved feeling. The feeling partner is not going to stop to consider the logic of every remark and action. Even the best of qualities tend to have inconvenient side effects, which may annoy those who do not see the reason for them, but the side effects are trivial in comparison with the good qualities from which they spring. When I was a child we had a neighbor who complained a great deal about her husband's faults. One day my mother asked her what she would really like to have changed in him. It took her some time to find an answer. Finally she said, "You know, there's that deep scar on his cheek. It doesn't bother me, but it bothers him."

It is the appreciation of what is fine in each other that matters, and communication of that appreciation, not necessarily in sentimental words. Some people comfortably assume their appreciation of their partner is understood; they should occasionally make it explicit. If it is too hard to be articulate about the big things, they can speak out about the small ones. "I like the way you laugh." "I looked across the room tonight and was so proud of you." "That was the best suggestion anyone made at the meeting." "You do think of the nicest things to do for people." What one says will be remembered.

Hostility can sometimes flare up suddenly between two people who love each other and neither may know why. Such clashes hurt less if both understand about the shadow side, which is visible to the partner but not to the possessor (see pp. 84–85).

Jung says that the acts of a person's shadow should not be taken as acts by the person. Obviously this is a difficult injunction to obey, but it is important in a marriage. If the behavior of a person's shadow is taken at face value, the partner may not only feel wounded and resentful, but the resentment may activate the partner's own shadow; to the serious detriment of the relationship, a bitter recrimination may ensue—not between the partners but between their shadows.

Such escalation is probably most serious in a marriage between two feeling types, where the eruption of the shadow is such an uncharacteristic violation of their harmony. The damage may be minimized, however, if they understand what is happening. When a person's shadow erupts, the partner may be able to recognize it as something not intended, and follow Jung's advice. The unconscious eruptions of the shadow cannot be prevented because a person does not know when they are going to happen; but if a person can catch an echo of what the shadow said or see the reflection of it in the partner's face, the person can make amends. "That was my shadow. I'm sorry."

There are several pitfalls to be avoided by a feeling type and a thinker married to each other. Feeling types should avoid being too talkative; one can easily talk too much to a thinker. Thinkers should not be too impersonal. They tend to think it obvious that by marrying a person they have demonstrated their esteem once and for all and that their useful everyday acts demonstrate their concern for that person's well-being (it would probably be a little sentimental to refer to it as happiness); therefore, it seems to them superfluous to mention either fact.

For example, one very busy NTP is careful to call home every evening when she is out of town on business. She inquires exhaustively about how things are going, because some problem may have arisen which she can solve. Eventually her ENFP husband changes the subject. "Aren't you going to say you love us?" It puzzles her that he needs to be told that she loves them. She wouldn't be worrying about these things if she did not love them! That, of course, is a logical inference that her husband could draw, but he does not want an inference. He wants to hear it said.

Feeling types want nourishment for their feelings. Thinkers are less concerned with feelings than with cause and effect. In order to avoid mistakes, they look ahead from a proposed action to its probable effect; that is a profitable precaution. They also look back from an unsatisfactory state of affairs to its probable cause, so that they may discover what mistake was made and try to insure that it will not be made again. When the mistake is their own, they benefit because they can change their own behavior as they see fit. If, however, they try to change their feeling partner's behavior by criticism, there is apt to be no benefit and a high cost. The feeling partner may react defensively, often at greater length than the thinker can tolerate with equanimity, and nothing is accomplished except frustration for the thinker and hurt for the feeling type.

If the thinking partner in a thinking-feeling marriage deeply wants some change in the feeling partner's behavior (something that will really make a difference to the thinker), the thinker's best approach is to avoid criticism altogether and simply express, as well as possible, the need and admiration for whatever it is the thinker desires. The feeling partner then has a valid incentive for making whatever effort is involved and doing it gladly. There is much nourishment for feeling in the thought that "My spouse likes me to do this!" but none at all in "doesn't like it if I don't." The first is an accolade for excellence, the second a reproof for falling below the norm. This approach will probably work better than criticism in any marriage. It makes no demand; it simply appeals for something— much desired—which the partner has the power to give.

Many of the thinkers' criticisms are not uttered with any expectation of producing change. They are just thrown out in moving from one thought to another. Even if thinkers are aware of their critical tendency and curb it discreetly in their working hours and social contacts, they (particularly TJs) will feel that at home they are entitled to blow off steam, forcibly, picturesquely, and with the TJ's characteristic exaggeration for the sake of emphasis. Among the targets of their casual criticisms may be the feeling type's friends, relatives, religion, politics, opinions on any subject, or merely something just told with an intent to amuse the thinker; and in this exaggerated form, the criticisms will not be true. The feeling partner will often be tempted to defend something or somebody against this undue severity. The temptation should be stoutly resisted.

For the sake of family peace, it is important for the feeling partner to learn the art of dealing with this "conversational criticism," which does not point out something that really should be corrected, but merely expresses the thinker's negative views ("I don't see how you can stand a featherbrain like Jones!"). The feeling partner needs to grant the thinker the luxury of expressing negative views without reprisals.

The feeling partner should not argue in defense of Jones, but will not wish to seem to concur. A relaxed laugh at the thinker's comment acknowledges the right of thinking to hold any opinion it pleases; a cheerfully casual comment such as "Jones has good points, too" reserves the same right to the feeling partner's own feeling, and the tone of voice dismisses the subject.

Someday the thinking partner may criticize so bluntly that it seems to take the very ground from under the feeling partner's feet. There are at least two possibilities other than that the feeling partner's world has come to an end. One is that the remark is a failure in communication; the thinking partner did not mean it the way it sounded, and does not feel the way the feeling partner would have to feel to say a thing like that. The other and more likely possibility is that it was not the thinker who said it. It was only the thinker's shadow.

In any marriage, a type difference may at times produce an outright conflict between opposite points of view. When this happens, the partners have a choice. One or both can assume that it is wrong of the other to be different—and be righteously indignant, which diminishes the partner. They can assume that it is wrong of themselves to be different—and be depressed, which is self-diminishing. Or they can acknowledge that each is *justifiably and interestingly* different from the other—and be amused. Their amusement may be warm or detached, wry or tender, according to their types, but it will help in working out the situation and keeping intact each partner's dignity and the precious fabric of their marriage.

CHAPTER 12

Type and Early Learning

THE MOST CONSPICUOUS relationship between type and education lies in the apparent advantage enjoyed by intuitives in most academic fields. They gravitate into higher education, as shown by the frequencies from the Type Tables in Chapter 3.

Both high scholastic aptitude and interest are found most often among intuitives. This is more than a fact. It is a promising clue to the mechanics of learning. What do intuitive children do that makes learning easier and more interesting? How could more children be helped to do it?

Translated literally from the Latin root, *intuition* is an inwardly directed watching. In type terminology, intuition is perception of the result of one's own unconscious processes. Just as the special province of sensing is the physical surroundings, the special province of intuition is the unconscious, from which insights come.

All children have the ability to perform specific operations very quickly on the unconscious level. They routinely use the unconscious to translate symbols into meaning or meaning into symbols as they talk, listen, read, and write. Another routine use of the unconscious is the retrieval of information from the memory; everyone has experienced a mental blank when communication between the conscious and unconscious suddenly fails and a desired name is completely inaccessible until, with equal suddenness, communication with the memory is restored.

Many uses of unconscious abilities are creative rather than routine. When children ask themselves "Why?" or "How?" they are asking for something previously unknown to their conscious mind—an insight that must be constructed unconsciously through a new combination of stored information. The request is made by the intuition, sometimes in its own search for relationships, interpretations, and possibilities, at

131

other times merely in the service of sensing, feeling, or thinking. Whatever the request, the intuition reads the product of the unconscious.

The reliability of symbols, memory, and insights depends on the adequacy of what is stored in the unconscious. A child's unconscious takes in three kinds of new materials: new information to be sorted, stored, and related to previously stored information; new insights to be transformed into principles, which enable the child to sort and relate new information and store it in a meaningful context; and specific questions requiring answers based on all relevant information and insights.

All new information that catches (or is forced upon) the child's conscious attention is used by the unconscious, but it does not necessarily remain available. To learn a new fact or idea, that is, to make it permanently accessible to voluntary recall, the child must give it enough attention to fix it in his or her mind. The required amount of attention is sometimes bestowed all at once, as in learning by experience that bees sting, but more often through gradual reinforcement, as in learning addition facts by rote or the meaning of new words from the context in which they occur.

How much attention the learning process requires in each case depends on the child's unconscious insights. If the child does not yet have the particular insight needed to make sense of the new information and to link it with what is already known, there is no context in which to store the new information. It goes into a limbo of separate and arbitrary facts, hard to understand, hard to remember, devoid of interest, and requiring an inordinate total of attention to be learned. If the child does have the insight needed to link up the new information with things already known, it can be learned permanently by paying only a modest total amount of attention and perhaps, if it is intrinsically interesting, surprising, or funny, with no effort at all.

Insights into general principles may come from external sources or from the child's own unconscious. Young children lack the stored information needed to generate many of the principles the unconscious applies. To learn at the best rate, every child needs help in acquiring the principles.

The earlier children are helped, the better. Although born with limited skills for processing information, in the first two or three years a child acquires more skills essential to intellectual development. By the age of three, one child may have established a pattern of meeting the unknown with eager comprehension; another may have accepted habitual noncomprehension as a way of life and not even care about understanding.

Foremost cognitive psychologists agree on the importance of the information that a child takes in during this earliest period. Studying brain physiology, Hebb (1949) distinguishes sharply between *primary learning,* by which the baby initially establishes the *autonomous central processes* presumed to underlie thought and account for intelligence, and the later learning made possible by these central processes once they are established. Piaget (1936), observing in detail the development of children's intelligence, finds that a baby's interest spreads out like ripples in a pond; the more new things that are seen and heard, the more new things the child will be interested in seeing and hearing. Bruner (1960), involved in nearly all aspects of education, includes in his research a study of how newborn babies learn to correlate perceptions. Hunt (1961) maintains that learning can be an engrossing sport; he describes the first couple of years as the most important, "so the idea is to do this from birth on—to manage the child's life in a way that will keep him interested as he goes along" (Pines, 1966, p. 48).

Consider what happens from birth on. In the first few days, an infant encounters information as separate, uncorrelated sensory impressions, and the first request to the unconscious is probably for a clue, any clue, to the meaning of all the blooming, buzzing confusion. If the unconscious can report that "there seem to be things that keep appearing," that insight becomes immediately useful on both the conscious and unconscious levels. Incorporated as an unconscious skill, it supplies the first rudiments of a way to organize information. New sensory impressions begin to be grouped around a few of the most distinctive "things that keep appearing." How something looks (from various angles) becomes linked with how it feels, tastes, and sounds; these pieces of information are stored together as material for future insights. From the baby's conscious standpoint, the insight into the existence of "things" helps break up the surrounding confusion into portions specific enough to consider. "What is all this?" becomes "What is that?" which is a more interesting problem and worthy of closer attention.

Here is the beginning of the baby's recognition of things and people. This skill comes sooner to the baby who has easily recognizable things to look at and handle, things that are big enough to be noticeable. A solid color is preferable to patches of colors, which tend to camouflage shape; solid color stands out against the background. Movement, too, distinguishes the object from the background and adds interest, even drama; babies love to watch a thing disappear and come back.

Seeing people correctly is harder for a baby than parents realize. Unlike Indian babies on their mothers' backs who see people right side up from the beginning, babies in cribs see people as horizontal objects. Babies on their backs see horizontal mothers leaning across them. On their sides, they see horizontal people walking up and down a vertical floor. (Readers can simulate this experience by tipping their heads ninety degrees.) Not until babies can sit alone do they usually have a good opportunity to see the world as they will see it for the rest of their lives. The images of family and environment that they have been constructing for six or seven months turn out to be all wrong.

With a little care, parents can make the baby's early perceptions correspond with reality. When babies are turned so their feet are toward the parent when they are changed, bathed, or dressed, the babies see the parent right side up. Babies who look in a mirror when they are burped will see themselves right side up on the parent's shoulder. When babies are old enough to hold their heads up, the parent can lay them on their stomachs and turn them so they have a view; in this position, they can see other people walking upright. In baby seats, too, they can see what is going on and develop a permanently valid set of images.

Another major insight that the unconscious uses to organize new information is that "particular happenings follow other happenings." A baby in our family learned before he was two weeks old that when he was snugly wrapped in a blanket he would soon be nursed. The minute the blanket began to go around him, he would stop yelling for his dinner and open his mouth for it. Once the baby subsconsciously understands a sequence of events, noteworthy sequences get filed away because they might be repeated. Those that consistently repeat give rise to fresh insights about the behavior of animate and inanimate things. On the conscious level, babies try out the idea of sequence on every event they can cause. "What will happen if I...?" The tenth time they throw their rattles out of the crib, babies may be watching to see if someone will pick it up this time, or they may be delighted that they *thought* it would hit the floor again and it did!

Here is the beginning of rational expectation and purposeful behavior. The rate at which babies develop expectation and intention depends largely on the variety and attractiveness of the events they themselves can bring to pass, which in turn depend on the variety and attractiveness of the materials to which they have access. Any object is interesting if it reacts to something babies can do—if, for example, it rattles when shaken or squeaks when squeezed or booms when thumped or dangling from elastic, snaps when let go or, best of all, makes light or darkness when pulled until it clicks.

Every such encounter not only adds to the babies' knowledge of how things behave but also helps to establish a lifelong belief that finding out is fun.

Before the dawning of language, the stimuli for finding out have to be physical or, as Piaget calls it, sensorimotor. Because direct communication is not yet possible, all new ideas or insights, which must be produced by the baby's unconscious, are limited to that which can be thought of in images or as other sense impressions.

A great step forward occurs when the major insight that "words have meaning" opens the way for speech. External speech permits communication; questions from children and answers, stories, and explanations from the parents extend children's experiences beyond the immediate environment. Internal speech permits children to talk to themselves; they can state thoughts and questions to their unconscious with a precision they could not achieve if they still had to think in images alone.

Maya Pines (1966) cites experiments in which "children as young as one to two-and-a-half who were told the name of the color red learned to find candy under a red cap much more easily than those who had no name for it; in fact, they required only one-third as many trials" (p. 187). Having a word for it helped them to concentrate on the one relevant detail. In another experiment, children were unable to pick out a pair of butterflies with similarly patterned wings until they were given verbal labels for the different patterns: *spots, stripes,* and so on. Thus, each word babies acquire brings an additional area of consciousness into sharp focus and increases their power to think about things—to observe, compare, categorize, and remember. A new word also increases their rate of learning, even on tasks involving no outward use of speech. Here verbal ability begins, and much depends on it.

The workings of the unconscious are more interesting to intuitive babies than to sensing babies from birth on. Intuitives therefore have more interest in the meaning of words and pay more attention to the words they hear. Because all children learn the meaning and use of words at a rate proportional to the attention they devote to words, sensing babies must give words the same amount of attention in order to develop verbal ability at the same rate as intuitives. To do so, the words must be sufficiently interesting by explicitly and actively relating to objects, experiences, or activities that interest the babies' senses.

Babies understand tone of voice before they understand the words spoken. When a voice does not sound interested, why bother to listen to it? But when the speaker sounds as if the words have an important bearing on the object presented, then the baby had better get it straight. Sure enough, the words do turn out to be important. Words for objects, words for actions, words for attributes, words for relationships—every word that babies can think to themselves crystallizes the reality it represents and makes that reality useful in mental operations.

As soon as communication is established, children no longer need to grope for all the insights, but can be told and shown the basic structure of life and experience. For example:

- *People have wants and needs.* These deserve respect. People should not interfere with each other's plans or possessions. Here begins the concept of the rights of others.

- *Things have uses.* Stoves to cook on, beds to sleep in, books to read, flowers to look at, all serve people's wants or needs in different ways. Here is the concept of value based on utility.

- *Things have to be made.* Or they have to be grown or raised or caught in the sea or dug out of the earth. Here is the concept of human effort as the mainspring of civilization.

- *Things have to be paid for.* When people want something that they cannot make or do not want to make for themselves, they must get it from someone else and pay for it. To earn the money to pay for it, they must do something useful that other people want done and are willing to pay for. Here is the concept of trade and the concept of money as a medium of exchange.

- *People work in hundreds of ways.* They work to get raw materials and to make things out of these materials. There is a story of work behind every familiar object in everyday use.

Children can understand these very simple ideas long before they can deduce the ideas independently. Once understood, the ideas produce a picture of a world of activity, where people constantly do and make useful things. To complete the picture, children need to understand the principles behind things.

One approach is to take the basic materials from which things have been made for thousands of years—stone, clay, wood, metal, glass, wool, cotton, and leather—and show the child not only what they are used for in daily life, but *why*. The hardness of stone, the ease with which clay and wood can be worked, the strength of metal and its ability to hold an edge, the transparency of glass, the tenacity of wool and cotton fibers when spun, the toughness and flexibility of leather—all are interesting facts in themselves. Taken together, these facts create a concept of the widely differing properties of matter, and they give the child new categories for classification and description.

From the obvious properties of materials, it is only a step to the ways materials can be changed. For example, high heat has dramatically different effects on different substances. Clay hardens, and then stands up against both fire and water. Metals grow red hot, then white hot, and then they melt; when they cool, they solidify, taking the form of the mold into which they have been poured. Organic plant and animal materials burn up and cannot be recovered. (Piaget says children are slow to grasp the concept of an irreversible process. It is important for the young to learn that destruction is irreversible.)

Next in interest after the raw materials are the basic steps by which they are made into usable things. These steps stand out most clearly in the original, primitive method of making something. When children picture themselves heating a piece of iron in a forge, first working the bellows to force air into the fire, then taking out the red-hot iron with a pair of tongs and hammering it into a hunting knife, they will remember the experience and the principles.

A good start on mechanical principles can be made by way of the ancient "simple machines." Each in its own way enables people to do work that is actually beyond their strength, and it does so by the device of stretching effort over a longer time or space. The underlying principles of lever, wheel and axle, pulley, screw, wedge, and inclined plane can be pointed out in familiar things. For example, the principle of the lever is demonstrated when the child slides to the end of a seesaw to balance a heavier playmate, or when a child opens scissors wider than usual in order to cut something thick.

The wheel and axle was widely used to haul buckets of water out of wells; the spokes of the wheel served as levers to make the axle easier to turn. The principles of the wheel and axle and of the pulley are the bases of the crane. Children see the wheel and axle at work in the steering wheel of a car and use it every time they turn a doorknob or the crank of a pencil sharpener.

The inclined plane was used to build the pyramids; today children use it to bicycle on a ramp from street level to a sidewalk.

An inclined plane wrapped around a cylinder makes a spiral screw. When it is turned, anything held between the threads must either turn with it or move along the spiral. Archimedes used that principle for lifting water out of the Nile. Today it is used to lift houses off their foundations, to adjust the height of a piano stool, and to hold the lid on a peanut-butter jar.

These principles have far-reaching importance. Understanding one principle in a new field gives children a foothold in that field. When they next encounter a related fact or idea, they can classify it mentally and relate it to what they already know. If they understand one principle in as many fields as possible, their knowledge, understanding, and *interest* can expand in all directions.

A principle of geography is that climate depends on how much the sun heats an area. Temperatures around the equator are very high because the sun shines straight down most of the year. Sunlight hits the polar regions on a long slant and loses much of its force; temperatures there are very low. Climates in between are more moderate and more pleasant. The difference in temperatures influences which crops people can grow and the way they build their houses. The contrasts between the bright noon sun and the dull red sunset and between summer and winter can give children an idea of the differences between climates.

Biological principles, which include the needs for food, water, air, and moderate warmth, bring up a host of interesting questions, such as why a scraped knee bleeds, why hunger increases after playing very hard, why thirst increases in summer, and why runners are out of breath after a race. And so on, through all the fields of knowledge.

CHAPTER 13

Learning Styles

"ONE OF THE great frustrations of teaching," remarked a teacher in a discussion about type, "is that you are always robbing Peter to pay Paul. You design something to reach one group of students, knowing that in so doing you are going to turn off another group. It is somewhat comforting to find that there is a perfectly understandable explanation." Thousands of teachers know this problem from personal experience. This chapter offers a logical interpretation of the problem and may suggest a method of attack.

Type makes a natural and predictable difference in learning styles and in student response to teaching methods. An understanding of type can help to explain why some students catch on to a way of teaching and like it, whereas others do not catch on and do not like it. Two distinct problems are involved here. Catching on is a matter of communication. Liking it is a matter of interest.

Communication from teacher to student begins with the spoken word in the classroom, where the student must be able to listen effectively, and later includes the written word in textbooks, which the student must be able to read. Because words, the necessary medium of education, have to be translated from symbols into meaning by the listener's intuition, the translation is naturally easier for intuitives than for sensing types. Intuitives use their favorite kind of perception, but sensing types have to use their less-liked, less-developed kind of perception, which takes more time and effort, especially when the words are abstract.

The first days of school are critical to the education of sensing children. Up to this time, they have focused their attention on the concrete realities around them, the things they can see, touch, and handle. Suddenly they are in a setting where they can *not* operate as usual. Everything seems to be words, some of which may not be familiar enough to be meaningful. And the words go by so fast. Children are often caught in the same predicament as adults who are trying to converse with a foreigner in the foreigner's language. Unfamiliar words take extra time to translate, and when the words go by too fast, translation becomes impossible.

It is fortunate that the teacher has control of how fast the words go by. Recognizing how much the sensing children need *time* to take in and understand words, the teacher can speak more slowly and pause after each sentence. Intuitive children will use the pause to add thoughts to what was said. Sensing children will use it to make sure they understand the teacher's words. Each sentence will then be a success in communication for all the children.

The children's ability to cope is at stake here. In the unfamiliar world of school, they deeply need to feel adequate, and the best way to feel adequate is to *be* adequate. If they genuinely do well in their required tasks by using their perception (to understand the task) and judgment (to do it right), they strengthen both for future use. The satisfaction of knowing something new or being able to do something new will provide inner motivation for further effort and further development.

However, if children consistently fail (or feel they are failing), the resulting discouragement may inhibit future effort and block not only the required learning but even more important, the development of the perception and judgment.

The habit of failure is extremely costly for the child, the educational system, and society as a whole. All reasonable precautions should be taken against failure. Required tasks should be simple and explicit, and they should make a definite contribution to the child's knowledge or skill. From the first day of school, the teacher needs to make it plain that there are many valuable and interesting things to be learned and there are reliable ways to learn them. Essential to any reading method is the reassurance that *letters stand for sounds* and, therefore, a printed word shows the reader what it would sound like if it were spoken.

Beginning readers should always be aware of the relationship between sounds and symbols. Of course, it comes very easily to some children, and they may use it before they begin school. If children know their letters and find out that letters stand for sounds, they can read as soon as they figure out the code. Children can match the letters and sounds by studying the spellings in a story or rhyme known by heart. They might point to a word printed on a book, newspaper, or cereal box and ask, "What does this say?" If their families do not answer, they ask a neighbor or the mail carrier. Every time children discover a new sound equivalent to a letter, they store it mentally.

With all the sounds and letters firmly in mind, children can read most of the words that are in their speaking vocabularies and many that are not. Coming across words they know but have not seen in print, they translate letters into sounds, sound out the word, and recognize it. After a few repetitions, they do not need to bother with separate sounds, but can translate the written word into the spoken word and eventually translate the written word directly into its meaning. For most unfamiliar words, the unconscious offers new readers a suggestion of what the word should sound like and a tentative meaning based on context. When a dictionary or other experience with the word establishes its meaning, children can read it correctly the rest of their lives without ever hearing it spoken.

The children who seem to teach themselves are those with a driving desire to read. Most children need help in learning the meaning (that is, the sound) of the symbols, and some children need a great deal of help. A growing number of schools are now teaching the sound-symbol relationships explicitly, letter by letter, from the start of first grade, so that children of all types can learn to deal confidently with the written word.

Some children, who do not have the luck to go to such schools, do not discover the principles of reading on their own or with their parents' help. They are expected to acquire a vocabulary of "sight words" before learning to sound out words. These children clutter their minds with false assumptions: that there is no good explanation of how to read, or surely the teacher would have given it; that a reader must find some way to remember each separate word—a task that gets harder the more one reads; and that there is no way to be sure what a word is until the teacher says it. They learn by the *word-attack method*, that is, they identify a word from its general shape or from its place on a familiar page or by remembering what comes next in the story or by looking at the nearest picture. None of these makeshift techniques is reliable in the actual reading of new material. They only obscure the real problem and its solution. The real problem is that the child who does not learn to translate letters into sounds can only "read" by memory and has no way to cope with new words.

The translation of sound-symbols is easiest for the introverts with intuition. In first grade the IN pupils are likely to be the quickest to catch on to the symbols and often are delighted with them. But the extravert children with sensing, the ES pupils, who make only minimal use of either intuition or introversion, may find the symbols so confusing that they become discouraged about the whole business of going to school. They may even decide, hopelessly or defiantly, that school is not for them.

Confusion about symbols is a very serious matter. Children of any type are doomed to flounder in school if they do not learn the meanings of the symbols by which language is written and must be read. They will be poor readers or nonreaders, depending on the depth of their confusion. They will do badly on achievement tests and intelligence tests. They will probably be bored by what they do not understand and may well be humiliated because they do not understand it. They tend to drop out of school as soon as possible. Their failures may be blamed on low IQ or perhaps on emotional difficulty, whereas actually the failures and the low IQ and the emotional difficulty could all result from one omission. Nobody helped them, in the beginning, to learn the explicit meaning of the sound-symbols.

In schools where the introduction of phonics is postponed, the sounds of the letters are eventually discussed, but only intermittently and as just one method of word attack among many. By this time the damage has been done and some students may be hopelessly behind. They cannot forget the old methods they used; they can only learn the new and store them side by side with the old. Of course, the new methods help, and the earlier they are learned, the more they help. But these children are not likely to become as skilled in the new methods as they would have with the right method from the start. For some children, the right method is too little and too late and never really works at all.

Communication from student to teacher, a relatively unrecognized aspect of education, has far-reaching consequences. It is needed whenever a teacher tries to find out orally or by a test how much students have learned or what they can do. When student-to-teacher communication is curtailed for any reason, it may leave the teacher with an unduly low estimate of the students' actual knowledge.

The speed with which intuitives translate words into meanings gives them an obvious advantage in any timed test of verbal ability or timed IQ test in which verbal ability figures. The extent of their advantage is evident when the scores of these tests are analyzed by type. Educational Testing Service made such an analysis on a large scale in the late 1950s before deciding to publish the Type Indicator (Myers, 1962). Among eleventh- and twelfth-grade students in academic courses at 30 Pennsylvania high schools, the average IQ of the intuitives topped that of the sensing types by 7.8 points for males and 6.7 points for females. Among male freshmen from five colleges, the mean SAT Verbal Ability score was 47 points higher for intuitives than for sensing students.

It is easy to assume that a substantial difference in native intelligence is indicated by such differences—about half a standard deviation, to put it statistically. That is far from the truth, however. Much of the sensing students' disadvantage on the tests is due simply to their test-taking technique.

For example, the ISFJ woman who thought she had to read every test question three or four times (see p. 59) was challenged by co-workers to take a parallel form of the test she had taken when applying for the job, but this time she would read each question only once. Although she agreed reluctantly, her second "IQ" score was ten points higher than the first.

Most sensing students who reread test questions at the expense of precious time *could* raise their scores by reading each question only once, but they are likely to be unwilling to try anything so rash. In effect, they do not trust their intuition to get the true meaning at first glance and, to an extent, they are right. Their reliance on soundness of understanding instead of quickness of understanding is a basic part of their strength and something to be respected rather than discouraged.

A fairer solution would permit sensing students to demonstrate their ability without having to violate their principle of making sure. By taking the time limit off the tests, teachers could turn them into power tests instead of speed tests. This solution does not lose or distort real differences in intelligence. Using the Wechsler as a standard measure of intelligence, Joseph Kanner (1975) explored the results of giving the Otis as a power test to two samples of over 400 students each. As ordinarily given, the Otis was expected to correlate about .49 with the Wechsler. As a power test, the r was .70 in one sample and .92 in the other. The results are hard to explain on any other ground than that the demand for speed obscures the true intelligence level as registered by the Wechsler.

Of course, speed is an undeniable asset in and beyond school. Both sensing and intuitive students might well benefit from exercises expressly designed to develop speed of response, but speed should not be confused with the *substance* of learning. Teaching methods should not make speed a prerequisite or a substitute for learning in general, and it should not be used to measure the extent of students' knowledge or the soundness of their reasoning.

Currently, reading teachers appear to be less concerned with the mechanics of reading than with comprehension of the material, that is, the use of higher levels of cognition, including logic and inference. The remarkable work of Dr. Mary Budd Rowe (1974a &1974b), of the Department of Childhood Education at the University of Florida, indicates that on these higher levels, too, a decrease in the demand for speed can produce an important improvement in results.

Dr. Rowe's study involved detailed analysis of over 300 classroom tape recordings of children in the early grades responding to science programs that were designed to provoke inquiry about nature. Two trends consistently emerged: The children's contributions were very meager, eight words in length on the average; and the pace of instruction was extremely fast. Teachers asked questions in rapid succession and waited an average of *only one second* for a child's answer before repeating or rephrasing the question, asking another question, or putting the same question to another child.

When children did answer but paused to frame their next sentences, teachers waited a little less than a second on the average before interrupting with comment or with another question. On the few tapes where the length and quality of children's responses were the kind that the programs were meant to encourage, the teacher had waited an average of about three seconds.

The findings of the first study led to larger scale studies of the consequences of persuading or training the teachers to wait three or more seconds. The results were impressive:

- The average number of words in a student's response was approximately quadrupled.

- The frequency of relevant statements volunteered was more than tripled.

- The frequency of responses showing inference from evidence was more than doubled.

- The frequency of speculative responses was more than tripled.

- Failures to respond were reduced from once in two minutes to once in fifteen minutes.

- A side effect, that teachers had few occasions for discipline, suggests that even the least scholarly children found the new proceedings more worthy of their attention.

One result that teachers had not foreseen was that they had a more favorable evaluation of some of the least promising students. After the teachers identified the five best and five poorest students in the class, the original tapes were scrutinized, revealing that teachers gave the five best students twice as much time to answer as they gave the five poorest. The teachers probably expected little or nothing from the poorest students, but with three seconds in which to respond, the bottom group began to answer in new and surprising ways, which were gratifying but inexplicable on the basis of their past performance.

From the standpoint of type, these changes are wholly explicable. The five poorest students would be sensing children who need more time to assimilate the substance of what they have heard. Even three seconds may make a large difference. It is exciting to speculate how much the performance of students in the lower half of a class might improve if they regularly had at least three more seconds in which to order their thoughts for expression. The advantage they would derive could extend far beyond the classroom into all the years of their lives.

In teaching, the other main problem related to type is the students' interest. Intuitives and sensing types differ greatly in what they find interesting in any subject even if they like, that is, are interested in, the same subjects. Intuitives like the principle, the theory, the why. Sensing types like the practical application, the what and the how. Most subjects have both theoretical and practical aspects and can be taught with the emphasis on either.

However a subject is taught, students tend to remember only the parts that capture their attention and interest. Theoretical presentations and assignments are likely to bore the sensing students. The practical side without the theory tends to bore the intuitives. A fifty-fifty mixture can be expected to bore everybody half the time. If students are allowed to spend most of their time on the aspects they will remember and find useful in their lives, there will be much more enthusiasm for education among its intended beneficiaries, and much more learning will take place.

In the textbooks of the future, an introduction to each chapter could present the essentials that all students must know in order to understand the aspects they will tend to find most interesting. The introduction could be followed by one section designed for sensing types and one for intuitives. Students could elect which to study, and either would suffice for credit. Exams would cover all three sections. Students would answer questions covering the introduction and the section of their choice. If some students studied all three sections, they could answer additional questions with the possibility of improving their grades.

Even without these textbooks, teachers can give students choices in assignments, projects, and even final exams. One teacher regularly supplies one group of questions for intuitives and others for sensing students and allows individual students to choose which they prefer to answer, as long as they answer a required number. Sometimes she permits students to compose a question that interests them and substitute it for one of hers. Many students, she says, do not take advantage of the permission. Perhaps they suddenly discover that it is more difficult to write a good exam question than they thought.

Teachers who are interested in type have at their disposal a laboratory for the observation of students' reactions to the classroom alternatives and for the formation of hypotheses based on those reactions. Programmed learning, for example, can seem restful to sensing students because it does not hurry them, and boring to intuitives because they cannot hurry it. One intuitive said that it would be all right if there were an "aha!" button he could push as soon as he understood.

At very young ages, the SN preference may show itself in ways that suggest useful alternatives. A second-grader who, according to his mother, was the only sensing member in their sizable family, was indifferent to reading and being read to. When she started reading him a child's history of actual events, his indifference was cured. "Did that really happen? Did people really *do* that?" His excited interest in real events confirmed that he had a need for indisputable reality. Of course, this is only one striking example, but it suggests that sensing children just starting to read may be much more interested if they are offered crisp facts, with a picture to go with each, instead of juvenile fiction or fairy tales.

A final word of warning may be in order. What is urged here is the use of interest as an aid to learning useful things, but never the acceptance of a *lack* of interest as an excuse for *not* learning things that need to be learned. The basic skills must be learned; the essentials for competence in an occupation must be learned.

When students are not interested in something that they must learn, they have two options. One is sheer application, which is not as prestigious as aptitude or as stimulating as interest, but it gets the job done. Application is most often used by J types, who run their outer lives with their judgment rather than their perception. Whether by chance or choice, the majority of sensing students are J. If they have the strengths of the judging type, they meet their deadlines and complete their undertakings, which is no mean achievement.

The other option was recommended to me at the age of four, in a conversation I remember word for word:

"Mother, what can I do?"

"Your closet needs to be straightened up."

"But I'm not interested in my closet."

"Well, *get* interested!"

That, in a nutshell, is the solution for students who find that application is a problem. There are a number of ways to get interested in an assignment, once the student takes a good look at it.

The assignment may be an exercise for improving some skill. If so, what is the skill? Is the student approaching it in the most efficient way? Can the student do it a bit better than last time?

The assignment may be an explanation of something. If so, just what is the point? Is it a complete explanation, or is the student being offered different viewpoints and left to choose the most reasonable?

The assignment may be an account of something the student may need to use someday. If so, how and when could it be used? What would have to be done to make it work?

Or the assignment may be some isolated name or date or rule the student is expected to remember. If so, would a rhyming couplet make it easier to remember?

In fourteen hundred ninety-two
Columbus sailed the ocean blue.

I before E
Except after C
Or when sounded like *aye*
As in *neighbor* or *weigh*.

Finally, if teaching that subject and making that assignment, what would *the student* do to make it more interesting?

CHAPTER 14

Type and Occupation

ONE ASPECT OF life that is observably influenced by type is the choice of occupation. A questionnaire given by Dr. W. Harold Grant (1965) to freshman classes at Auburn University contains this highly perceptive question:

What do you consider the most important feature of the ideal job?

(a) Provides an opportunity to use one's special abilities

(b) Permits one to be creative and original

(c) Enables one to look forward to a stable and secure future

(d) Provides one with a chance to earn a good deal of money

(e) Gives one an opportunity to be of service to others

The five types that favored the stable and secure future were all sensing types. The warmest of the sensing types, ESFJ, characteristically favored service to others. Seven of the eight intuitive types favored either the opportunity to use their special abilities or the chance to be creative and original. The sensing types were thus less concerned with the nature of the job than with its stability, given which they expected to find or develop their own sources of satisfaction. The intuitives wanted to find fulfillment in the job itself, preferably by doing something creative. Dr. D. W. MacKinnon (1961) of the Institute for Personality Assessment and Research found that especially creative groups, whether architects, writers, research scientists, or mathematicians, are almost entirely composed of intuitives.

The preference that seems to have the most influence on occupational choice, the SN preference, determines in large part what will
interest people. Sensing types are drawn to occupations that let them
deal with a constant stream of facts, whereas intuitives like situations in
which they look at the possibilities.

The next most important preference is TF, which determines the
kind of judgment that is easier and more agreeable to use. People who
prefer thinking are more skillful in handling matters that deal with
inanimate objects, machinery, principles, or theories—none of which
have any inconsistent and unpredictable feelings and all of which can be
handled logically. Feeling types are better skilled in matters involving
people, what they value, and how they can be persuaded or helped.

When people tentatively choose an occupation, they should carefully consider how much use the job would make of their own preferred
kind of perception and kind of judgment; prospective workers in any field
should find out all they can about what they will be doing and how much
time will be spent on each kind of work. Although no job is perfect, it is
easier to accept the imperfections cheerfully if the job gives workers the
opportunity to use their preferred processes.

People who are completely open-minded about occupations can
benefit from looking at the kinds of work that appeal most to people with
the same best-liked perceptive process and judging process. Each of the
four possible combinations of perception and judgment tends to produce
distinct interests, values, needs, and skills. Figure 33 shows the range of
frequencies from 0 percent to 81 percent for fifteen groups.

ST people focus their attention on facts and handle these with
impersonal analysis. They tend to be practical and matter-of-fact, and
they successfully use their abilities in technical skills dealing with facts,
objects, and money. In the sample of accountants, 64 percent were ST,
and among the finance and commerce students and bank employees, ST
made up 51 percent and 47 percent, respectively. STs also do well in
production, construction, applied science, and law, but among the
samples of counseling and theology students, only 6 percent and 3
percent were ST.

SFs also focus their attention on facts, but they handle these with
personal warmth. They tend to be sympathetic and friendly, and they
enjoy occupations that provide practical help and service for people. In
the sales and customer relations sample, 81 percent were SF, and among
nursing and education students, SFs accounted for 44 percent and 42
percent. SFs do well in medical specialties involving primary care,

Figure 33. Distribution of Types
Within Occupational and Academic Group

	ST (%)	SF (%)	NF (%)	NT (%)
Occupations				
Accountants	<u>64</u>	23	4	9
Bank employees	<u>47</u>	24	11	18
Sales, customer relations	11	<u>81</u>	8	0
Creative writers	12	0	<u>65</u>	23
Research scientists	0	0	23	<u>77</u>
Fields of Graduate Studies				
Theology (liberal)	3	15	<u>57</u>	25
Law	31	10	17	<u>42</u>
Fields of College Studies				
Finance and commerce	<u>51</u>	21	10	18
Nursing	15	<u>44</u>	34	7
Counseling	6	9	<u>76</u>	9
Science	12	5	26	<u>57</u>
Health-related professions	13	36	<u>44</u>	7
Education	13	<u>42</u>	39	6
Journalism	15	23	<u>42</u>	20
P.E. and health	32	34	24	10

Sources: MacKinnon (1962) and Laney (1949)

health-related professions, community service, education (especially elementary), and physical education. But among students of law, counseling, and science, SFs made up only 10, 9, and 5 percent.

The very high frequency of SFs in sales and customer relations illustrates the powerful effect that type can have on turnover. In studying the types of Washington Gas Light's employees, Laney (1949) originally analyzed the preferences separately, not in combination. Nine years later, in preparing the table shown in Figure 33, we asked for the complete types and found the company had discarded the records of those no longer employed. Almost four-fifths of the feeling types were still there, but almost four-fifths of the thinkers had quit (Myers, 1962).

NFs prefer possibilities to facts, and they handle these with personal warmth. Often their enthusiasm and insight bring them success in understanding and communicating with people. In the samples of counseling students and creative writers, 76 percent and 65 percent were NF; among students in theology, the health-related professions, and journalism, the percents of NF were 57, 44, and 42. NFs also do well in teaching, research, and literature and art; but among the finance and commerce students, sales and customer relations people, and accountants, NFs made up only 10, 8, and 4 percent.

NT people also focus their attention on possibilities, but handle these with impersonal analysis. They tend to be logical and ingenious, and they often use their abilities in theoretical and technical development. Among the research scientists sampled, 77 percent were NT; and among the science and law students, 57 and 42 percent were NT. NTs also do well as inventors, managers, forecasters, and securities analysts. In four of the fields studied, the NTs represented only a small percent: They made up 9 percent of the accountants and of the counseling students, 7 percent of students of nursing and the health-related professions, 6 percent of education students, and none of the sales and customer relations people.

People should not be discouraged from pursuing an occupation because they are "not the type." When an occupation is seldom chosen by people of their own type, the prospective workers should investigate the job thoroughly. If they still want to pursue it and are willing to make the effort required to be understood by their co-workers, they may be valuable as contributors of abilities that are rare among their co-workers. For example, among the correctional officers in a Florida prison (Bogart, 1975), there were very few intuitives, not more than 12 percent, but when a training course in human relations was instituted to aid the officers in rehabilitating prisoners, the rare intuitives developed a higher level of skill than did the sensing types. Another example is an ESTJ clergyman, a type so rare among the clergy that we inquired how he functioned. The answer was, "He gets mortgages paid off. As soon as the mortgage is burned, he moves on to another parish with another mortgage."

When people find a field of interest that uses their best skills, there is usually a considerable variety of work in that field. Here the EI preference may be important. Although everyone lives partly in the extravert world of people and things and partly in the introvert world of concepts and ideas, most people are consciously more at home in one of those worlds and do their best work in the preferred world.

Among ST people, for example, the introverts (IST) enjoy organizing facts and principles related to a situation; this is an important part of the work involved in economics and law. The extraverts (EST) like to organize the situation itself and get it moving, which is particularly useful in business and industry.

Extraverts tend to be more interested and effective when things are happening all around them and they are working actively with objects or people. Introverts tend to be more interested and effective when their work involves ideas and requires a good deal of their activity to take place quietly inside their heads.

Part of considering a specific job, therefore, is understanding how much extraversion the job requires (of an introvert) or permits (for an extravert). Some people go very easily back and forth between extraversion and introversion; they may find most satisfaction in jobs involving considerable amounts of both, but most people are happier when their work lies mainly in the world they know best.

The EI preference also can have a powerful effect on turnover. Laney's study (Laney, 1949, & Myers, 1962) showed that among men with IQs above 100, turnover for extraverts working in the quiet, clerical jobs was nearly double the turnover for extraverts working in the active jobs as mechanics or meter readers; and introverts who were working in the active jobs were nearly twice as likely to quit as introverts working in the quiet, clerical jobs.

The JP preference can affect satisfaction. J people do their extraverting, their handling of people or situations, mainly with their best judging process, thinking or feeling, as the case may be. P people do their extraverting mainly with their best perceptive process, sensing or intuition. Accordingly, J types and P types approach situations quite differently.

Judging types, especially those who prefer sensing (the SJ types), like their work to be organized, systematic, and foreseeable—often to the point of knowing what they will be doing next Thursday at three o'clock. Perceptive types, especially those who prefer intuition (the NP types), want their work to be a response to the needs of the moment. Jobs differ greatly in these respects.

Jobs also vary greatly in the number of decisions demanded in the course of a day. Judging types, especially those who prefer thinking, tend to see the power to decide as an enjoyable feature of a job. Perceptive types, especially those who prefer feeling, often find routine decisions a burden and would rather *see* their way to a solution than deliver a crisp choice between alternatives. It is not surprising, therefore, that in a sample of school administrators 86 percent were J (von Fange, 1961), and in a sample of students in counseling education 64 percent were P (see Chapter 3, Figures 23 and 19).

Figures 34 and 35 list some of the many respects in which people who are opposite on a given preference tend to differ in their reactions

Figure 34. Effects of the EI and TF Preferences in Work Situations

Extraverts	Introverts
Like variety and action.	Like quiet for concentration.
Tend to be faster, dislike complicated procedures.	Tend to be careful with details, dislike sweeping statements.
Are often good at greeting people.	Have trouble remembering names and faces.
Are often impatient with long slow jobs.	Tend not to mind working on one project for a long time uninterruptedly.
Are interested in the results of their job, in getting it done and in how other people do it.	Are interested in the idea behind their job.
Often do not mind the interruption of answering the telephone.	Dislike telephone intrusions and interruptions.
Often act quickly, sometimes without thinking.	Like to think a lot before they act, sometimes without acting.
Like to have people around.	Work contentedly alone.
Usually communicate freely.	Have some problems communicating.

Thinking Types	Feeling Types
Do not show emotion readily and are often uncomfortable dealing with people's feelings.	Tend to be very aware of other people and their feelings.
May hurt people's feelings without knowing it.	Enjoy pleasing people, even in unimportant things.
Like analysis and putting things into logical order. Can get along without harmony.	Like harmony—efficiency may be badly disturbed by office feuds.
Tend to decide impersonally, sometimes paying insufficient attention to people's wishes.	Often let decisions be influenced by their own or other people's personal likes and wishes.
Need to be treated fairly.	Need occasional praise.
Are able to reprimand people or fire them when necessary.	Dislike telling people unpleasant things.
Are more analytically oriented—respond more easily to people's thoughts.	Are more people-oriented—respond more easily to people's values.
Tend to be firm-minded.	Tend to be sympathetic.

Figure 35. Effects of the SN and JP Preferences in Work Situations

Sensing Types	Intuitive Types
Dislike new problems unless there are standard ways to solve them.	Like solving new problems.
Like an established way of doing things.	Dislike doing the same thing repeatedly.
Enjoy using skills already learned more than learning new ones.	Enjoy learning a new skill more than using it.
Work more steadily, with a realistic idea of how long it will take.	Work in bursts of energy powered by enthusiasm, with slack periods in between.
Usually reach a conclusion step by step.	Reach a conclusion quickly.
Are patient with routine details.	Are impatient with routine details.
Are impatient when the details get complicated.	Are patient with complicated situations.
Are not often inspired, and rarely trust the inspiration when they are.	Follow their inspirations, good or bad.
Seldom make errors of fact.	Frequently make errors of fact.
Tend to be good at precise work.	Dislike taking time for precision.

Judging Types	Perceptive Types
Work best when they can plan their work and follow the plan.	Adapt well to changing situations.
Like to get things settled and finished.	Do not mind leaving things open for alterations.
May decide things too quickly.	May have trouble making decisions.
May dislike to interrupt the project they are on for a more urgent one.	May start too many projects and have difficulty in finishing them.
May not notice new things that need to be done.	May postpone unpleasant jobs.
Want only the essentials needed to begin their work.	Want to know all about a new job.
Tend to be satisfied once they reach a judgment on a thing, situation, or person.	Tend to be curious and welcome new light on a thing, situation, or person.

to various work situations. Because the reactions are general, they cannot describe every individual in every situation, but they can be expected and understood in light of type theory.

For example, introverts derive their faculty for concentration, at least in part, from their tendency to pay more attention to what is going on inside their heads than to what is going on around them. This is a great help when the workers' productivity depends on their ability to keep from being distracted by the people around them. At the First Pennsylvania Bank in Philadelphia, the extraverted supervisor of the central transcription department was asked to rate her typists on the quantity and quality of their work; she gave higher ratings to the eight introverts than to any of the eight extraverts (Laney, 1946–1950).

The same department had had trouble finding satisfactory messengers. Their responsibilities included bringing cylinders from all over the bank and carrying finished work back to the point of origin. In the intervals between runs, messengers maintained the stock of supplies for the typists. After two highly unsatisfactory messengers had worked in the department, the other members of the department wanted Personnel to explain why they were having such difficulty in finding a good messenger. Personnel asked what characteristics were required for the job and found there were no prior ideas on the subject.

Personnel then asked for the names of the two unsatisfactory messengers together with a detailed description of their shortcomings, and for the names of messengers whose work had been satisfactory. Type Indicators from the files suggested a tentative explanation. The complaint against the most current offender was that she made a social occasion of every errand: She talked too much and too long and with too many people, including the typists. Her type was ESFJ—and the standard temptation for ESFJs is talking too much. The other offender's fault was that she became so determined to do what she had planned to do, that she was unconcerned with running the errands. Her type was ISTJ—and ISTJs are very hard to deflect from the job at hand, a trait that is a virtue in most circumstances. Of the satisfactory messengers, one was an ESFP who had progressed to typist and on to secretary, and the other an ISFP who had left business to enter a convent.

On this slender evidence, central transcription decided to try an SFP with S for awareness of detail, F for desire to comply with expectation, and, above all, P for adaptability to the needs of the instant. Personnel sent to central transcription the next SFP applicant who came along, and central transcription was delighted. They reported that the new messenger always kept track of what was most needed at the moment and could remind the typists that "this is the stuff that Mr. Ratchett is in such a rush for" in such a nice way that Mr. Ratchett's work got back to him in record time. In this fashion one case, too small to be a statistic, can add up to the knowledge both of a job and of a type, and it can become a statistic if confirmed by subsequent observation.

In another department, credit investigation, the supervisor was constantly critical of the workers who made inquiries by telephone. She complained that after they had called the same source a few times they initiated an acquaintance with the voice at the other end; she wanted Personnel to send her someone who would not digress from business. The Indicator showed that the supervisor was T and the workers were F, so that their ideas of business would never coincide with hers. Personnel looked for a worker with T and sent over an ENTP, who would have been most unsuitable for routine clerical work. The supervisor declared the new worker was the best credit investigator the department had ever had.

Information about type can also be gathered from cases in which a person is unsatisfactory in one job and succeeds when shifted to another. An INTP whom the bank acquired through a merger seemed to be a misfit in every department where he was tried. No supervisor wanted to keep him. At last there was a vacancy in securities analysis, which the personnel department had been waiting for. The INTP was transferred there and has had top ratings ever since.

Of the 22 accountants in a utility company who were supervisory grade or higher, only three were intuitives, and not one of the three was satisfied or satisfactory where he was (Laney, 1946–1950). In an effort to improve the situation, the executive-type intuitive (ENTJ) was made Assistant Comptroller; in this job his organizing ability and his ideas for improving procedures mattered more than his personal accuracy with clerical detail. Within two years, he was offered the job of Comptroller with another company—a happy outcome for him, if not for the original company.

The analytical-type intuitive (INTP) was made Assistant Trea-surer; in his new position he worked on complex projects like pension plans and completed the work with great satisfaction to the company and to himself. After the third one (INFJ) destroyed the morale of his subordinates by demanding unnecessary rechecking (seen by them as overperfectionism), he was asked to leave. The personnel department concluded that "intuition *and* feeling are just too much in accounting."

Testimony from a worker well suited to his occupation comes from an INTP who is assistant transportation manager of a large oil company. Questioned on his work, he described it as a jigsaw puzzle job involving "constant adaptation to shifts in variables," that is, selection of whatever combination of methods of transportation would be most economical for each shipment. He added, with a most unusual freedom of expression for his type, "Don't know anything that's more fun."

Nippon Recruit Center in Tokyo (1977) has for many years used a Japanese translation of the Type Indicator for better placement of workers in business and industry; their experience suggests that the basic relationships between type and occupation transcend the boundaries of language and culture. Frequencies of the preferences in four contrasting occupations ran true to type theory. For example, half of the office supervisors in a city bank were ES. After mentioning the steadiness and realism of the S types, the Japanese commentator added, "They can also endure positive and fixed duties." Among factory workers doing skillful repetitive work, 85 percent were S, which the commentator regarded as evidence that "this kind of job has no relationship with abstractions." The sample of copywriters was predominantly ENP; among the telecommunication technicians doing research planning, N and T types were in the majority and the INT types were five times as frequent as in the other groups.

Much of the occupational data has been gathered from students preparing for careers. In his study of art students (Chapter 3, Figures 16–18), Stephens (1972) found marked differences in type between those who intended to be artists, those who wanted to teach art, and those who planned to use art in therapy. The artists were predominantly IN types capable of following their inner creative urge without much reference to the outer world. Most of the therapists were EF types bent on using art to help people in trouble. There is little overlap between these two groups, one oriented to creativity and the other oriented to people; but the group between, those who want to teach art and communicate to others their knowledge and understanding of beauty, are predominantly NF types who share the artists' attraction to creativity and the therapists' attraction to people.

In law school (Chapter 3, Figure 21), type affects not only who gets in but also who drops out. Miller (1965), in a study of law students from prominent schools, found that dropout had no significant relation to the standard predictors of success (college grades and admission test scores) but *was* related to type. TJ types did best at both arrival and survival, whereas FP types tended to do poorly at both. The types in between, TP and FJ, both dropped out at a rate moderately worse than average, but there were twice as many TPs as FJs.

Medicine is the occupation for which the relationship between type and career choice has been studied most intensively. Over 4,000 medical students who took the Type Indicator in the early 1950s have been followed up, first in the early 1960s from data about their specialties in the 1963 directory of the American Medical Association (Myers & Davis, 1965) and again in the 1970s in a much more inclusive study for the Department of Health, Education, and Welfare by a clinical psychologist at the University of Florida and Director of the Center for Applications of Psychological Type (McCaulley, 1977).[13]

Prior to any follow-up, the operations of self-selection were apparent. More introverts, intuitives, feeling types, and (to a lesser extent) perceptive types were found among the medical students than could be expected in a general collegebound group of students in the 1950s. The different frequencies could be predicted from the twofold appeal of medicine. A physician may be a scientist, a humanitarian, or both. The humanitarian side of medicine gives full play to the warmth of feeling. The scientific side is suited to the intuitive's zest for problem-solving, the introvert's gift for concentration, and perceptive type's inclination to find out everything about what is wrong before treating it.

The net result of this self-selection is that high school graduates with all four of the predisposing preferences, INFPs, are at least four times as likely to enter medical school as classmates with the four opposite preferences, ESTJs. The combination of intuition and feeling apparently furnishes the strongest motivation, perhaps because medicine presents problems to solve for the benefit of *people*.

By far the least attracted type was ESTJ, the businessman and businesswoman type, in which all four preferences correlate with business interests on the *Strong* and economic values on the AVL *Study of Values*. Apparently the high financial rewards in medicine, which should have special interest for an ESTJ, did not offset that type's relatively low interest in the scientific and humanitarian aspects of the work itself.

Type seems to affect the drop-out rate, the percentage of students who permanently quit or fail medical school.[14] In this sample, a relationship was found between drop-outs and the nature of the dominant process—judging (EJs and IPs) and perceptive (EPs and IJs). Although the mean Medical College Admission Test scores for the perceptive students and the judging students were identical, the perceptive types had a drop-out rate of 3.1 percent, whereas the judging types had a drop-out rate of 5.0 percent. Perhaps the perceptive students have more accurate perceptions of themselves and their careers and, therefore, make more suitable choices, which are less likely to result in failure or quitting. The highest drop-out rate for any type in this study was 7.0 percent for ESTJ, the type that was least attracted to medicine to begin with.

ESTJ also had a larger proportion of its members in general practice than any other type, although it is not a type to which the role of devoted family doctor would be expected to appeal. Before the first follow-up study, general practice was suggested in the 1962 Indicator Manual as suitable for the warm-hearted types with sensing and feeling; psychiatry and teaching for the insightful types with intuition and feeling; and surgery for the objective types with sensing and thinking. The types themselves confirmed the hypotheses by choosing these fields with significant frequency. The prevalence of the "hard-hearted" ESTJs in general practice would thus seem to come less from enthusiasm for that field than from impatience to start earning money—without the delay of up to five years of residency.

In the first follow-up study of specialty, the greatest difference was in the kind of perception preferred. Whereas the sample as a whole was 53 percent intuitive, psychiatry was 82 percent intuitive, research 78 percent, neurology 76 percent, medical faculty 69 percent, and pathology 68 percent. In all these fields, introversion was also preferred, but to a lesser degree. These complex fields appeal to the intellectual approach of the introvert and to the problem-solving ability and tolerance for the complicated that characterizes the intuitive.

The opposite types, the extraverts with sensing, preferred surgery and obstetrics. These specialties demand maximum sensory awareness of physical conditions from moment to moment. Both demand skill in action, which is the extravert's forte. Extraverts with sensing chose obstetrics twice as often as did introverts with intuition, and surgery half again as often.

The Type Table of specialties in Figure 36 shows the significant attraction of the sixteen types to specialties, research, and medical faculty positions. For example, pediatrics appealed highly to ESFJ, in whom the feeling of SF is the extraverted process and therefore more apparent.

The corresponding intuitives, ENFJs, were the types most attracted to full-time teaching in medical school. They, too, nurture the young, but attend to the intellectual needs of the young adults rather than the physical needs of children.

Anesthesiology made its strongest appeal to ISTP and ISFP; their acute SP watchfulness is reinforced by the introvert's capacity to

Figure 36. Attraction of Specialties to Each Type (Ratio of Actual to Expected Frequency of Specialties Within Each Type)

Sensing Types

With Thinking		With Feeling	
ISTJ		**ISFJ**	
Pathology	1.74	Anesthesiology	1.76
Obstetrics, Gynecology	1.46		
Psychiatry	.44		
ISTP		**ISFP**	
Anesthesiology*	2.05	Anesthesiology	1.84
Psychiatry*	.39	General Practice*	1.40
Pathology	.33		
ESTP		**ESFP**	
Surgery	1.38	Obstetrics, Gynecology	1.44
Psychiatry*	.25	Medical Faculty	.43
		Psychiatry*	.33
ESTJ		**ESFJ**	
General Practice**	1.46	Pediatrics	1.51
Internal Medicine	.68	Psychiatry**	.16
Psychiatry*	.36		

Intuitive Types

With Feeling		With Thinking	
INFJ		**INTJ**	
Internal Medicine	1.42	Neurology*	2.75
		Research**	2.72
		Pathology*	1.99
		Internal Medicine*	1.44
INFP		**INTP**	
Psychiatry**	2.04	Neurology*	2.35
		Research*	1.98
		Psychiatry**	1.84
		Pathology*	1.78
		Obstetrics, Gynecology**	.44
ENFP		**ENTP**	
Psychiatry*	1.52	General Practice	.70
General Practice	.73		
ENFJ		**ENTJ**	
Medical Faculty	1.69	Internal Medicine	1.35

Note: *significant at .01 level; **significant at .001 level; others significant at .05 level concentrate for a long time. Anesthesiology does not appeal to the other SP types, ESTP and ESFP, perhaps because their extraversion tends to shorten their attention span.

Pathology and research were both notably popular with INTJ and INTP, who have in common the three preferences most conducive to detached intellectuality. Pathologists and medical researchers can cope with life-and-death problems without seeing a patient face to face.

The first follow-up study could show nothing about the satisfaction afforded by the choice of specialties. The second follow-up, which examined *changes* in specialty, showed how often doctors of each type changed to a more typical specialty (to one more generally chosen by their type) and how often to one less typical. The results strikingly confirmed the conclusion suggested by the answers of the Auburn University freshmen that sensing types either know much less or care much less than do intuitives about the suitability of any given job for their type (see p. 149).

Among those who changed specialties, the sensing types changed to a more typical specialty only 54 percent of the time, which is little better than chance, whereas the intuitives changed to a more typical specialty 71 percent of the time. As usual, ESTJ and INFP presented an extreme contrast. The ESTJs changed to a *less* typical specialty 68 percent of the time, which suggests that the change may have been dictated by external circumstances and not by their liking for the work itself. The INFPs changed to a *more* typical specialty 83 percent of the time; of all the types, they appeared to care most about a chance to use their gifts.

Especially pleasing was a remark made by an unforgettable person. She was the head of a school of nursing, serenely lovely in the white habit of her order. With her eyes on the Type Table, she listened attentively to a two-minute explanation of type. Then putting her finger on ESTJ in the lower left corner, she said, "These are the administrators."

She was right, but how could she have known? She must have looked at the four letters of that type, selected from the brief explanation the salient characteristics associated with each letter, and put them together into a recognizable portrait: attention focused on the outside world; respect for facts and capacity for detail; judgments based on cause and effect; and immediate decision—administrators.

Ideally, co-workers constitute a team with a common purpose and should work for the same general goal. Their differences in type can be an asset because they help people to do and to enjoy widely different kinds of work. One job may be boring or confusing to one type and hence badly done, but it could be interesting and rewarding to another type and expertly handled. A person can be a failure at the wrong job and outstanding at the right one. For example, introverts with intuition first think of new possibilities simply as ideas. Extraverts with intuition translate ideas into action, but they do not have much interest in carrying the action beyond the point where everything is worked out. Sensing types, however, take great satisfaction in producing tangible results and providing against circumstances that would interfere with production.

Thinking types tend to be particularly effective in jobs dealing with inanimate objects (which can be changed by force), and feeling types tend to be good at dealing with people (whose cooperation cannot be forced but must be won). Sensing types with the judging attitude function well and contentedly in structured jobs with sharply defined procedures that must be followed, but intuitives with the perceptive attitude chafe at such jobs, where they cannot take the initiative to pursue the possibilities they perceive.

Any team, therefore, should include a sufficient variety of types to perform the required jobs effectively and with satisfaction. Cooperation, however, can run into difficulties because people of opposite types often disagree on what should be done, or how, or whether anything needs to be done at all. Such disagreements are natural: Opposite kinds of perception make people see different aspects of a situation, and opposite kinds of judgment direct action toward different ends. If the disagreements are not resolved, they can damage team morale and effectiveness and diminish job satisfaction, regardless of how suitable the jobs are.

Morale and effectiveness will survive intact if the members of the team recognize that both kinds of perception and both kinds of judgment are essential to a sound solution of a problem. The prescription for individually solving a problem is to exercise all four processes in succession: sensing to establish all the facts, intuition to suggest all the possible solutions, thinking to determine the probable consequences of each course of action, feeling to weigh the desirability of each outcome in human terms. An individual is handicapped in doing this because the less-liked perception and judgment are relatively immature and therefore not as helpful as they might be, but a well-balanced team of individuals should include at least one skilled representative of each process.

By considering the contributions of each member, the team or its executive head can make a more informed decision than would otherwise be possible. As a further aid to cooperation, these contributions demonstrate that each member is weak where another is strong but is also strong where another is weak. A healthy respect for one's opposite makes for peaceful and effective coexistence. It also helps in recognizing and cultivating one's own less-developed processes.

Communication between different types is a greater problem than is generally recognized. A statement that is clear and reasonable to one type may sound meaningless or preposterous to another. One married couple, having learned how their types differed, proudly reported their insight. "If we argue for fifteen minutes without getting anywhere, we go back and define our terms. We haven't been talking about the same thing!"

To be useful, a communication needs to be listened to, understood, and considered without hostility. It is natural for people not to listen attentively when they expect that the communication will be irrelevant or unimportant. Therefore, it should begin with a topic sentence that promises something worth listening to. Of course, what is deemed interesting varies from type to type, but the presentation of a good idea can usually be designed to suit the listener's interests. Sensing types, who take facts more seriously than possibilities, want an explicit statement of the problem before they consider possible solutions. Intuitives want the prospect of an interesting possibility before they look at the facts. Thinkers demand that a statement have a beginning, a logically arranged and concise sequence of points, and an end—especially an end. And feeling types are mainly interested in matters that directly affect people.

A communication may be listened to and understood but still fail its purpose if it arouses antagonism. Thinkers are the people most likely to fall into this trap because they tend to be bluntly critical, but feeling types also consider themselves justified in attacking something that seems wrong. Any attack is likely to provoke spirited defensiveness and lead to a divisive struggle between colleagues instead of a united attack on the problem. If the dissenter will refrain from condemning the incomplete solution and simply stress the unsolved part of the *problem*, the others can consider the dissenter's comments with no loss of face and can broaden or change their solution accordingly. This technique works whether or not members of the group know each other's types.

PART IV

Dynamics of
Type Development

CHAPTER 15

Type and the Task of Growing Up

THE ESSENCE OF type development is the development of perception and judgment and of appropriate ways to use them. Growing up is much easier with adequate perception and adequate judgment. By definition, people with adequate perception see the relevant aspects of any situation; if they also have adequate judgment, they make good decisions and carry them out. Whatever problems young people may face, adequate perception and judgment make it possible to face the problems in a mature and creditable manner It is worthwhile, then, to consider how type theory and type research may contribute to the development of these faculties.

Types differ fundamentally in the kind of perception and the kind of judgment they *can* best develop. These preferences are inborn and no attempt should be made to reverse them; otherwise development may be blocked. Knowledge of type should be used to encourage and to increase opportunities for members of each type so they can develop in their own directions to the peak of their own powers.

Type research has shown that the types differ in their interests, values, and needs. They learn in different ways, cherish different ambitions, and respond to different rewards. The present system of public education succeeds with particular types but fails to bring many students to a satisfactory state of maturity.

The possible effects of research and type theory on fostering maturity can be considered from two lines of attack. One is to research what motivates the different types in practical situations. The more that is known about what matters to each type, the easier it is to predict which objectives will most fully enlist their energies in the growing-up years. The second is to study the normal course of type development from babyhood through adulthood, in order to discover what circumstances enhance the development of perception and judgment.

167

Van der Hoop's discussion of the stages of type development does not include the ages at which they may be expected to occur.

> In every type there is a simple form, in which the differentiation of the prevailing function has only just begun, and its modes of adaptation are still being tentatively tried out, although a clear preference for typical forms of adaptation can already be observed. At a later stage the dominating function has found its forms, controlling these with great assurance. Anything which is not in accord is, at this stage, suppressed. With a few people there follows a still further stage, in which the other functions are permitted more development, to compensate for any one-sidedness, and the pronounced typical picture is again modified to some extent by the unfolding of a fuller and richer expression of human nature. (1939, p. 92)

The last stage comes only to people who live their type fully but continue growing. Through the completeness of their type development, they come face to face with the inevitable deficits of their particular type. Without abandoning the values of their best-developed processes, they can use their self-understanding to recognize and cultivate the values of the previously neglected third and fourth processes. Thus, they ultimately transcend their type. This is admirable, but if it is attempted *before* the person has achieved full development of the best two processes, it may merely divert the person from that development and have a negative effect.

Type development starts at a very early age. The hypothesis is that *type* is inborn, an innate predisposition like right- or left-handedness, but the *successful development* of type can be greatly helped or hindered by environment from the beginning.

Probably the most deeply rooted preference, and the one that appears earliest, is that for extraversion or introversion. Even an infant may show a decided bias in favor of the sociable or the contemplative life. In three-year-old twin sisters whose environment has always been identical though the twins are not, the difference between the extravert and the introvert may be obvious to the most casual beholder. Their needs will be different, too. The extravert needs plenty of action, people, variety, conversation, and opportunity to make a satisfying amount of noise. She is a part of all that she has met, and her grasp of the world depends on *how much of it* she has met. The introvert can use the same things, but not in such quantity. Too much togetherness leaves her drained. She needs a place where she can be alone and quietly concentrate on what interests her. For her sense of security, she needs to be told about the underlying principles that hold the world together, even when her parents think she is much too young to understand. She will be much more at home in the world that seems to be held together, rather than a world that seems to lie around in unrelated pieces.

The TF preference, and the resulting family conflicts, can also show up at a very early age. A six-year-old feeling type said in dismay after a week's visit from a five-year-old thinker, "He doesn't care about *pleasing*, does he?" Basically, he does not. He has to have reasons. The young thinker, even at two years old, will do things for reasons but sees no point in doing them for love. The young feeling type will do things for the sake of pleasing but is unmoved by logic. To be influenced, thinking types and feeling types must be motivated by something meaningful to their own type. If no one shows appreciation of young extraverted feeling types, they may behave obnoxiously just to get a reaction so they can be in contact with others. If no one gives young thinkers reasons to consider, their thinking will spend itself largely in dissent and be labeled negativism.

The SN preference can show up early, too. The sensing child is enchanted with what is; the intuitive with what is not, or at least not yet. "The Little Man Who Wasn't There" is a strictly intuitive conception. Imaginative play, fairy tales, fiction of all sorts, fascinating new words hoarded away with half-guessed meanings for future delight—these nourish the intuitive child's zest and wonder. But the intuitive child born into a very matter-of-fact family, who has no time for books and no talk about anything except obvious realities, will go half-fed.

Sensing children vastly prefer actuality. They get satisfaction out of "really" cooking or tinkering like their parents and are tirelessly interested in things that can be touched and handled, taken apart and put back together, but not at all in things that seem to have no existence except in words or other symbols. Sensing children are likely to dismiss Mother Goose as silly when they ascertain that the cow did not, in fact, jump over the moon.

By the time children reach seventh grade, their types can be identified with a useful degree of accuracy by the Type Indicator. From then on, the degree of type development prevailing in a group can be roughly assessed by using the split-half reliability of the Type Indicator scores. Each scale is split into equivalent halves and the results from the two halves are compared. The more consistently the responses are governed by type, the greater will be the agreement between the halves and the higher the reliability.

Although no direct criterion of maturity is available, the split-half reliabilities, taken as reflecting a sample's general level of type development, can be used to compare the relationship between type development and a particular indirect indicator of maturity. This approach was used in studying the records of three junior-high samples, which differed widely in achievement. Because maturity is an important factor in achievement, the three samples probably represented three levels of maturity. The groups were similar in having an above-average IQ, and on EI and JP, they showed average reliabilities equal to those of college-prep twelfth-graders, which suggests that the junior-high students had EI and JP preferences as well established as older students able to do college-prep work.

On SN and TF, however, the reliabilities for the three groups varied in an interesting way. The first group, potentially collegebound seventh graders with IQ above 107, had markedly lower reliabilities on SN and TF than the group of twelfth-graders. This suggests that the perceptive process and the judging process are not ordinarily as well developed in seventh-graders as they will be five years later.

The second and third groups had higher IQs. The second group consisted of gifted students (IQ of 120 and above) in the seventh to ninth grades, with very high achievement. Their reliabilities on both SN and TF were as high as those of the group of twelfth-graders. This suggests that they had attained an early development of both perception and judgment.

An alternative explanation is that the second group might have higher SN and TF reliabilities simply because of their higher IQ, but this explanation is negated by the evidence of the third group. The third group was composed of underachieving eighth-grade boys with IQ above 120. They produced a very low reliability on TF—much lower than that for the first group, the potentially collegebound seventh graders. The very low reliability on TF suggests a marked immaturity of the judging process, that is, a deficit of judgment.

It is reasonable that perception and judgment should be harder to develop than mere attitudes and that judgment often seems to be the hardest part of growing up. The first group, the regular seventh-graders, presumably had reached a level of perception and judgment that was normal for their age and intelligence. The gifted students who made up the second group gave evidence of *more* than routine maturity of perception and judgment when all members of the group scored high on all the standard achievement tests they took; such results do not automatically follow from a high IQ but require a superior accomplishment of a number of requirements. The third group, the underachieving eighth-grade boys, failed to meet even those requirements that were well within their abilities and thereby gave evidence of *less* than routine maturity.

This evidence suggests that the Type Indicator split-half reliabilities on SN and TF, when taken as a measure of the average maturity of perception and judgment in a group, could be used in determining which curricula and teaching methods contribute most to growing up.

The evidence also indicates that there are wide differences in type development between groups of effective people and groups of ineffective people and that these differences can be detected as early as seventh grade.

Some of the reasons for such differences are examined in the following chapters.

CHAPTER 16

Good Type Development

EVERY TYPE HAS its good and bad examples, its happy and unhappy people, its successes and failures, saints and sinners, heroes and criminals. Different types are likely to go wrong from different angles. When an introvert smashes a moral principle, it may well be knowingly and in bitterness. The intuitive extraverts, in the grip of a project, and the judging extraverts, with their set purposes, may consider that the end justifies the means. (The end may sometimes be unselfish, as with the woman—undoubtedly a feeling type—who stole from her employer to give lavishly to the needy.) The types most prone to *drift* into wrong-doing, from a thoughtless yielding to circumstances or bad companions, are the extraverted sensing types. In extreme cases, they may have neither enough introversion or intuitive insight to warn them of the underlying principle involved nor the judgment with which to criticize their impulses.

As described in Chapter 9, general patterns of behavior can be attributed to each of the sixteen types, but the strengths of each type materialize only when the type development is adequate. Otherwise, people are likely to have the characteristic weaknesses of their type, but not much else.

Essentials of Good Type Development

In normal type development, a child regularly uses the preferred process at the expense of its opposite and becomes increasingly skillful in its use. More and more able to control the favorite process, the child acquires the traits that belong to it. Thus, the child's type is determined by the process that is used, trusted, and developed most.

Although the favorite process can be useful by itself, alone it will not be healthy, safe for society, or ultimately satisfying to the individual, because it lacks balance.

The dominant process needs to be supplemented by a second process, the auxiliary, which can deal helpfully with the areas that the dominant process necessarily neglects. The auxiliary process must supply the needed perception if the dominant process is a judging one, or vice versa, and must contribute the needed extraversion if the dominant process is primarily introverted, or vice versa.

Good type development, therefore, demands two conditions: first, adequate but by no means equal development of a judging process and a perceptive process, one of which predominates; and, second, adequate but by no means equal facility in using both the extraverted and introverted attitudes, with one predominating.

When both conditions are met, the person's type development is *well balanced*. In type theory, *balance* does not refer to equality of two processes or of two attitudes; instead, it means superior skill in one, supplemented by a helpful but not competitive skill in the other.

The need for such supplementing is obvious. Perception without judgment is spineless; judgment with no perception is blind. Introversion lacking any extraversion is impractical; extraversion with no introversion is superficial.

Less obvious is the principle that for every person one skill must be subordinate to the other and that significant skill in any direction will not be developed until a choice between opposites is made.

Necessity for Choice Between Opposites

Expert perception and judgment result from specialization, from using one of a pair of opposites rather than the other. One of the opposites must be "tuned out" in order to have a chance to develop either of them.

Trying to develop skill in sensing and intuition at the same time is like listening to two radio stations on the same wave length. People cannot hear an intuition if their senses are dinning in their ears, and when listening for an intuition, people cannot get information from their senses. Neither kind of perception is clear enough to be interesting or worth sustained attention.

Similarly, if people cannot concentrate either on thinking or on feeling, their decisions will be made and unmade by a shifting dispute between two kinds of judgment, neither of which is expert enough to settle matters permanently.

The four processes *are* used almost at random by very young children, until they begin to differentiate. Some children begin differentiating much later than others, and in the least-developed adults, the processes remain childish, so that nothing can be maturely perceived or maturely judged. Even in effective adults, the two least-used processes remain relatively childish, and the effectiveness lies mainly in the two processes which have grown skilled from being preferred and exercised.

Difference in Rank of the Two Skilled Processes

The two skilled processes can develop side by side because they are not antagonistic. One is always a perceptive process and the other a judging process, so they do not contradict each other. Although one can assist the other, there should be no doubt about which comes first.

The supremacy of one process, unchallenged by the others, is essential to the stability of the individual. Each process has its own set of aims, and for successful adaptation, as Jung pointed out, the aims must be "constantly clear and unambiguous" (1923, p. 514). One process needs to govern which way a person moves; it should always be the same process, so that today's move will not be regretted and reversed tomorrow.

Therefore, of the two skilled processes, one must be the "General," and the other must be the "General's Aide," attending to lesser but necessary matters which the General leaves undone (see pp. 12–14). If the General has a judging nature, the Aide must supply perception as a basis for judgment, but the Aide of a perceptive General needs to provide decisions to implement the General's vision. The Aide to an extrovert must do most of the reflecting, whereas an introvert's Aide will have to take action.

In the extravert, other people meet and do business with the General. Staying in the background, the Aide shows little on which others can evaluate his competence. In the introvert, the General works inside the tent, while the Aide takes care of business with others.[15] If the Aide is skillful and competent, the General need not be called on. If the Aide is awkward, help from the General may be needed.

Results of Inadequacy
of the Auxiliary Process

In addition to a clear choice of which two processes will be developed and which of the two will dominate, good type development requires adequate use of the chosen processes. The auxiliary naturally tends to be neglected. Extraverts, in using their dominant process in the outer world, may not know that they need the auxiliary.

In Judging Extraverts

Judging extraverts with insufficient perception may never discover their lack. Making decisions without adequate information, they will make mistakes but will be unable to "perceive" their responsibility for their misfortune. Because these E—Js cannot distinguish between good and bad decisions, they may feel as competent to decide other people's affairs as their own and thereby make many of their mistakes at other people's expense.

They are unable to see the individuality of persons and situations; they fall back upon assumptions—prejudices, conventions, stereotyped attitudes, and common misconceptions. Living in a world of clichés, they derive a sense of security by using one cliché or another to dispose of practically anything. Within such limits, their exercise of judgment may be prompt, consistent, and resolute, but it will be no better than their assumptions. Anything that refutes their assumptions and demands an unfamiliar effort at perception will shake their security.

In Perceptive Extraverts

Perceptive extraverts who do not develop judgment have the opposite deficits, which often get them into extraordinary difficulty. They do not know what is best to do, so they do not take any action. Or they know what they should do, but cannot make themselves want to do it, and, therefore, they do not do it. Or they want to do something and know they should not, but cannot stop themselves. Often they do not even bother to ask themselves whether they should or should not take a particular course of action. Frequently they are likable, charming people, but because they have no judgment, they do not deal firmly with their difficulties, and they shy away from difficulties. They tend to consider work a difficulty.

In Introverts

Because the auxiliary process is what introverts use in dealing with the world, they are more likely than extraverts to develop an adequate auxiliary. If they do not, the results are painfully conspicuous and awkward; all their contacts with their environment will be clumsy and ineffective. If they manage only an inadequate development, they will still be at a disadvantage when dealing with the average extravert in the world of action—though they will have a compensating advantage in the world of ideas. Some introverts develop an auxiliary process without learning how to extravert it. In this fashion, they get balance in their inner lives, but no satisfactory extraversion.

Rewards of Good Type Development

When the essentials of good type development are achieved, the advantage is great. Observation has convinced the authors that type development is a variable with a wide range and profound influence on effectiveness, success, happiness, and mental health.

The extent to which type is developed affects not only the value of the inborn type but also the value of the inborn intelligence. Within limits, type development can *substitute for intelligence,* because average intelligence, fully utilized through fine type development, will give results far above expectation. However, a serious deficit of type development, especially a deficit of judgment, constitutes a disability for which no amount of intelligence can compensate. In the absence of judgment, there is no assurance that the intelligence will be brought to bear upon the necessary things at the necessary times.

Especially for introverts, a modest improvement in balance, brought about by taking the contributions of the auxiliary process more seriously, may pay large dividends in satisfaction.

Practical Pursuit
of Good Type Development

Type development is aided by clear choice between the opposites and purposeful use of the chosen processes. The first step for people examining their choices and use of the chosen processes is to see for themselves the difference between each pair of opposites and to discover which processes and attitudes serve their deepest needs and interests and thus are fundamentally right for them.

The next step is to see the difference between the appropriate and inappropriate use of each process. An appropriate use of sensing is for seeing and facing the facts, and intuition is appropriately used for seeing a possibility and bringing it to pass. Thinking is the process best suited for analyzing the probable consequences of a proposed action and deciding accordingly, and feeling is best for considering what matters most to oneself and others.

Each process can be used inappropriately, too. Examples of inappropriate use include indulging sensing by running away from a problem to a trivial amusement, giving in to intuition by dreaming up impossibilities that would provide an effortless solution, indulging feeling judgment by rehearsing how right and blameless one has been all along, and yielding to thinking judgment by criticizing anyone who has an opposite view of a problem. Such behavior would put the four processes to use but without accomplishing anything.

In practicing the use of all four processes, people frequently find that only one of the four is easy to exercise. For example, some people feel comfortable only with sensing, or only with intuition, and uncomfortable with both kinds of judgment. This is most likely to happen in the case of an extreme perceptive extravert and would suggest too little development of judgment.

The first step toward more satisfactory type development for extreme perceptive extraverts is to realize that they are used to operating almost exclusively in the perceptive attitude, with practically no use of a judging process. Consequently, they are extremely responsive to outer circumstance, which may be a new situation, person, or idea. Thus influenced from without, rather than governed by definitive standard or purpose from within, the extreme perceptive extraverts lack continuity and direction. They are blown about like a sailboat whose master has forgotten to drop the centerboard.

The centerboard is judgment, that is, a disciplined power of choice in accord with permanent standards. If thinking is the judging process, the standards will be impersonal principles. If judgments are based on feeling, the standards will be very personal values. Either way, well-developed standards enable their possessors to act in a pattern consistent with long-term desires.

Therefore, if you are an extreme EP, you need to recognize and establish your standards, apply them to your choices *before* acting, and act accordingly.

How your standards are established depends on your TF preference. If you prefer thinking, you are generally aware of the law of cause and effect, even though you have not been applying that principle to your own affairs. With effort, you can probably make a good guess at why particular things in your life have not gone as well as you wanted, and you can probably see what you should have done differently. You can even predict to a useful degree the consequences of your actions.

If you prefer feeling, you need to make a conscious examination of your feeling values. The standards of feeling judgment are personal values, which are arranged in the order of their importance. In considering an action, weigh the values that will be served against the values that will suffer. By taking the course that serves the values that matter most to you in the long run, you will insure that the decision will continue to content you.

Of course, no one can prescribe another's hierarchy of values. In choosing a job, does comfort or freedom matter more to you? Would you rather have security or an unfolding possibility with no guarantee attached? Does it seem to you more important that people should be well fed, well clothed, well taught, healed, amused, or stimulated—and into which of these endeavors would you prefer to pour your energies? If it is a question of your dealings with people, would you rather be liked for your charm or trusted for your sincerity? If it is a question of the use of the next ten minutes, is it more rewarding to start something new or finish something old? Every problem raises its own questions, and the questions most relevant to your problems can be answered only by you.

CHAPTER 17

Obstacles to Type Development

THE BASIC TYPE differences *appear* as differences in interest, but the division goes very deep and rests on a natural tendency to develop in a particular direction and a natural desire for particular goals. Successful development in the natural direction yields not only effectiveness but emotional satisfaction and stability as well, whereas the thwarting of the natural development strikes at both ability and happiness.

If the direction of the development were entirely dependent on the environment, there would be nothing to be thwarted, but, in fact, a main hazard to good type development is the opposing pressure of environment.

Pressures of Environment

The finest examples of type development result when children's immediate environment encourages their native capacities. However, when an environment squarely conflicting with their capacities forces children to depend on unnatural processes or attitudes, the result is a falsification of type, which robs its victims of their real selves and makes them into inferior, frustrated copies of other people. The greater the original possibilities, the greater the frustration and strain of unfulfillment. Jung says that "as a rule, whenever such a falsification of type takes place as a result of external influence, the individual becomes neurotic later.... A reversal of type often proves exceedingly harmful to the physiological well-being of the organism, often provoking an acute state of exhaustion" (1923, p. 415).

If, in fact, some people are born without any inner disposition to be one type or another, then outer circumstances, one might conjecture, would have a free hand in determining which (if any) attitudes and processes would be developed. Western civilization has inclined men toward thinking, women toward feeling, and both sexes toward extraversion and the judging attitude. The pressure of outer circumstance itself would seem to be toward sensing. Thus, anyone who came into the world as a clean slate would be likely to be marked ESTJ or ESFJ fairly promptly by the collective slate pencil, which may explain why there are so many ESTJs and ESFJs in the general population.[16]

Against that view, type theory would argue that readiness to accept and enforce conformity is an essential part of the inner disposition of ESTJs and ESFJs. Thus, the prevalence of these types could be a cause, not a result, of some of the more materialistic social pressures of our times.

Lack of Faith in One's Own Type

The less-frequent types find their infrequency an obstacle to their development. In the general population, there may be three extraverts to every introvert and three sensing types to every intuitive. Although the percentages of introverts and intuitives is much higher in college-bound and college-educated groups, outside these groups the introvert with intuition is about one in sixteen during the formative years of primary and secondary school (see Chapter 3, Figures 4 and 6). Unless the introverts with intuition are stoutly skeptical of the mass assumption that a difference is an inferiority, their faith in their type will diminish. They will not trust and exercise their preferences, which, accordingly, will not be developed enough to be beneficial. These people are thus cheated out of the successful undertakings that would give them faith in their type. Introverts with sensing, although less seriously outnumbered, are subject to much the same difficulty.

Lack of Acceptance at Home

If parents understand and accept their children's type, the children have a spot of firm ground to stand on and a place in which to be themselves. But if children suspect that their parents want them to be different—to go against their own type—then the children lose hope.

When parents have a little explicit knowledge of type they can give introvert children a new lease on life. The children will not find it a daunting undertaking to learn how to extravert *when necessary* if they know that they are always free to be introverts. Although children are far more vulnerable, even grown-ups can have their faith in their own type undermined by the beloved person who does not understand or accept it.

Lack of Opportunity

A more obvious hindrance to development is simple lack of opportunity to exercise the favored processes or attitudes. Unknowingly parents frequently refuse their children the conditions necessary for good type development: the young introverts who get no peace or privacy, the extraverts shut off from people and activity, the intuitives tied to routine matters of fact, the sensing children required to learn everything through words with nothing to see or handle, the young thinkers who are never given a reason or permitted an argument, the feeling types in a family where nobody cares for harmony, the judging types for whom all decisions are handed down by an excessively decisive parent, and the young perceptives who are never allowed to run and find out.

Lack of Incentive

Lack of incentive often curtails type development. Growth is a stretching process, and children do not stretch their perception or their judgment until they try to do something *well*.

The moment children begin to take seriously the quality of their performance, they try to see into the situation or the problem as completely as possible. In so doing, children stretch their best perceiving process. If this process is sensing, they focus on the facts, and if it is intuition, they concentrate on canvassing the possibilities; either way they develop their perception. Then having seen as much as possible, they try to choose the soundest way of taking action, and this effort stretches their best judging process. If this process is thinking, they work to foresee the logical results of everything they might do. If it is feeling, they weigh the personal values involved—their own and other people's. In either case, they develop their judgment.

None of this happens, however, unless children have good reason for wanting to do something well, which leads to the basic problem of motivation.

CHAPTER 18

Motivation for
Type Development in Children

THERE IS AN immense observable difference between people who are happy and effective and people who are neither. Much of this difference can be ascribed to the quality of their judgment. If *good judgment* is the ability to choose the better alternative and act accordingly, then the judgment of happy, effective people must on the whole be reasonably good and the judgment of ineffectives must be fairly bad.

Good judgment is achieved by a lifelong effort to find and do the right thing in whatever situations arise. Thus, whether or not children develop judgment depends on what they do about problems and dissatisfactions. For children who absolve themselves of all responsibility and make no effort, the type development stands still; but for children who cope with problems, the type development progresses.

Children who cope become increasingly able to face and solve problems and are led by this skill to competent maturity. Children who reject the challenge to change unsatisfactory states will find themselves in worse and worse situations as life gets more complicated; demands and responsibilities increase, but their ability to handle problems does not. Unlike the upward spiral to maturity, which requires an effort aimed beyond the impulse of the moment, the downward spiral is easy to slip into, because it involves doing only what the individual pleases. Undeveloped people would rather do as they please than make such an effort, and all children are undeveloped to begin with. For children to get started on the upward spiral, they must be motivated to make the effort.

What children need is the conviction that *satisfaction can and must be earned.* Parents who value this conviction can give it to their children, but the parents must start early and remember both the "can" and the "must."

185

Spoiled children do not learn the *must*. They get what they want, regardless of what they deserve. If their parents give in to tantrums, the children get what they want by *not* deserving it. They get no first-hand experience of cause and effect in the adult world, nor any practice in judging the worth of their conduct as the world will judge it. They are not even warned that the world will judge.

Spoiled children are therefore conditioned to blame all their troubles on an outside cause. If they are not liked or trusted, or if they get low grades, it does not occur to them to work at being more likeable or trustworthy or studious. Everything bad that happens to them is no fault of their own. Seeing no reason to make an effort at development, they make no effort and do not develop.

At the other extreme are children who are underindulged, unloved, repressed, and discouraged; they may not learn that satisfaction *can* be earned. If nothing they do is ever right or successful or applauded, they may take refuge in doing as little as possible.

Because both spoiled children and discouraged children lack the incentive necessary for development, their perception and especially their judgment remain childish. Years later, physical maturity arrives without psychological maturity. What had seemed to be only a child's refusal to try to meet relatively simple requirements of home and school can become a devastatingly complete inability to meet the demands and responsibilities of adult life.

Essential to a fortunate childhood, therefore, is a just and easily understood relationship between children's conduct and what happens to them. When youngsters follow simple rules (with a large, merciful allowance for accidents, misunderstandings, and a reasonable amount of forgetting), the consequences should be approval, confidence, and the perceptive attitude from grown-ups. As an earned bonus, children should have the largest feasible measure of freedom to make their own decisions. When children knowingly do the wrong thing, the consequences should be consistently disagreeable. Under such conditions, they learn to obey the spoken word and the known rule in the same spirit that they obey the law of gravity, under a similarly mild but inevitable penalty, and at the same age, fifteen months or younger.

Recognizing as a fact of life that it is more profitable to find and do the right thing than the wrong, children have incentive for *discriminating* between the right thing and the wrong thing in their own conduct and *doing* the right thing even though it is less pleasant, less attractive, or less interesting at the moment. This is the beginning of judgment.

Once children start on the upward spiral of development and growth, the effects are cumulative. When better behaved, children are increasingly acceptable to other people, especially their own families, and can be admitted to many more privileges and opportunities for development. In general, whatever they do will prosper. When it does not prosper, they study what they did wrong, because experience has taught that doing something right will bring about success. If after honest scrutiny they cannot find anything, they are able to stop worrying because they know from experience that all they need to do is their best.

One satisfaction that youngsters can earn is an earlier and easier emancipation from parental authority. If children have continuously been taking responsibility, their parents are not afraid to give more of it. Such children are ready to grow up.

Youngsters on the downward spiral, however, have been taking no responsibility, and the prospect of having to grow up is at least unconsciously terrifying. Many adult neuroses may be due to childhood spoiling, not childhood trauma. A sense of guilt or incompetence is a logical enough consequence of failure to develop. In undeveloped people who could and should have developed, the lack of development cannot be explained as due to a long-past experience that is "no fault of their own." Such people need to get the process of development running at last under its own power. Guilt can be a useful part of that power mechanism if the feeling convinces them that they should be doing something better. It forces them to make the effort to find out what they should do, and sees them through doing it.

Unfortunately, the inner resistance against making the effort seems to be proportional to the amount of effort required. Well-developed types find it relatively easy to heed the warning signal of guilt or misgiving and to alter their behavior because their perception and judgment are trained for the purpose. People with a severe type deficit, especially a deficit of judgment, seem to build an immense resistance not only against making the effort but even against admitting that the effort should be made.

Popular lines of defense include the following: "There is no use trying, because I cannot do the required thing," which runs the gamut from mere inferiority feelings through disabling physical symptoms, such as actual hysterical blindness and paralysis. "The required thing is not worth doing." In this situation education may be labeled bunk, manners criticized as an affectation, and any worker scorned as a sucker. "I have done the required thing, but I have been cheated of what I deserve." Here the defensive person may claim that the teacher is partial, the kids run in cliques, the coach does not give anyone a chance, the boss plays favorites, or the system is unfair.

Defenses can block effective dealing with a problem because they prevent the necessary first step, recognizing that one has probably been doing something wrong. If the defenses have become habitual, the person has quit trying and is committed to the downward spiral.

However, *children can be convinced* from the beginning that satis-faction can and must be earned. Both home and school should provide them with the experience of *doing particular things well* and thereby earning the satisfaction they crave. Because the various types have different gifts and needs, the specific things they do well and satisfactions they crave cannot be the same for all children.

Schools that abolish report cards in order to avoid hurting the feelings of the poorer scholars are on the wrong track. To promote development, schools should not disregard excellence but diversify its recognition by rewarding nonacademic excellences as well, preferably those that do not depend on intuition.

The mother of a six-year-old came to a similar conclusion and acted on it with a touch of genius. She realistically saw that if her son was to have an outstanding quality, it would have to be developed from scratch. She chose persistence. Her son had no interest in persisting, but he was very fond of marshmallows. For a "good finishing day," his ration was two marshmallows; for a "very good finishing day," he got three; and for special achievements, four. At first, of course, his mother had to be his judgment, but the incentive was sufficient to focus his attention on the difference between good finishing and poor finishing. Eventually his own judgment took over; it became part of everything he did and won him a distinguished reputation for dependability.

Type development is fostered by excellence in almost anything that children can, with effort, do well. As Jung once said, if they have planted a cabbage right, they have saved the world in that spot. The excellence need not be competitive, except as children try to excel their own past performance, and *virtue need not be its own reward.* The sat-isfaction earned by the striving can be whatever furnishes the strongest incentive to the child, for example, extra pleasures or possessions for a sensing child, special freedoms or opportunities for an intuitive, new dignity or authority for a thinker, and more praise or companionship for a feeling type.

Every time children earn satisfaction, they are moved farther along the upward spiral of development. The effort involved in doing something well exercises perception and judgment and leaves the children better equipped for the next problem; each satisfaction they have *earned* strengthens their faith that effort is worthwhile. As children grow into the unindulgent adult world, where everything really satisfying must be earned, they are prepared to earn their own satisfactions.

CHAPTER 19

Going On
From Wherever You Are

I WROTE THIS final chapter long after the rest of this book was written and laid aside. The intervening years have shown me, more and more vividly, how great a contribution the understanding of type can make to people's lives. Whether people first hear about the two kinds of perception and two kinds of judgment as children, high school students, parents, or grandparents, the richer development of their own type can be a rewarding adventure for the rest of their lives.

Ten years ago I was less confident, Had this book been published then, it would have ended with the previous chapter and might have given the impression that type development runs on a time table and must be achieved by a particular age or not at all. I do not think now that that is true. Good type development can be achieved at any age by anyone who cares to understand his or her own gifts and the appropriate use of those gifts.

Whatever stage people have reached, a clear understanding of the basics of type development will help them to go on from there. As has been said throughout this book, almost everything people do with their minds is an act of perception or an act of judgment. Succeeding at anything takes both perception and judgment and in that order. Before people can rightly decide how to handle a situation they must find out what the problem is and what the alternatives are. Finding out is an exercise of perception, and deciding is an exercise of judgment. To be sure of using perception *before* judgment, people must understand the difference between the two and be able to tell which one they are using at a given moment. The latter skill can be acquired by practice in small matters. For example, when people wake in the night to the sound of rain and think, "Why, it's raining hard," that is perception. If they then think, "I'd better check if it's raining in!" that is judgment.

Of the two very different kinds of perception, sensing is the direct perception of realities through sight, hearing, touch, taste, and smell. Sensing is needed for pursuing or even casually observing hard facts; it is equally essential to enjoying the moment of a sunrise, the crash of surf on a beach, the exhilaration of speed, and the smooth working of one's body. Intuition is the indirect perception of things beyond the reach of the senses, such as meanings, relationships, and possibilities. It translates words into meaning and meaning into words whenever people read, write, talk, or listen; people use intuition when they invite the unknown into their conscious minds or wait expectantly for a possibility, a solution, or an inspiration. Intuition works best for seeing how situations might be handled. A thought that starts "I wonder if" is probably intuition. The declaration "I see!" is a flash of intuition, and the thought "Aha!" indicates that intuition has brought to mind something enlightening and delightful.

If people prefer sensing, they use it more and become expert at noticing and remembering all the observable facts. Because of their ever-growing fund of experience and knowledge of reality, sensing types tend to become realistic, practical, observant, fun-loving, and good at working with a great number of facts.

People who prefer intuition tend to become skilled at seeing possibilities. They learn that a possibility will come to them if they confidently seek it. Valuing imagination and inspirations, intuitive types become good at new ideas, projects, and problem-solving.

One kind of judgment, thinking, is logical and intentionally impersonal; it does not include *all* ingenious mental activity, much of which, in fact, is the product of intuition. Thinking analyzes in terms of cause and effect, and it distinguishes between true and false. The other kind of judgment, feeling, is intentionally personal and is based on personal values. It distinguishes between valued and not valued and between more valued and less valued, and it guards whatever the feeling type values most. Although feeling judgment is personal, it is not necessarily egocentric, and at its best, it takes into account the feelings of others as far as they are known or can be inferred. Feeling should not be confused with emotions; in fact, Jung calls it a rational process.

Thinking types become most skillful in handling that which behaves logically (like machinery) with no unpredictable human reactions. Thinkers themselves tend to become logical, objective, and consistent; they are inclined to make decisions by analyzing and weighing the facts, including the unpleasant ones.

Feeling types, who develop skill in dealing with people, tend to be sympathetic, appreciative, and tactful; in making decisions, they are likely to give great weight to the relevant personal values, including those of other people.

The four processes—sensing, intuition, thinking, and feeling—are gifts that all people are born with. The processes are at each person's disposal to develop and use in dealing with the present and shaping the future.

The Individual's Road to Excellence

It is up to each person to recognize his or her true preferences—between sensing and intuition, between thinking and feeling, and so on. According to type theory, the preferences are inborn, but just as parents frequently try to make a left-handed child right-handed, they may try to convert a sensing child to intuition, or a thinking child to feeling, to conform to the *parent's* inborn preference. Unless stoutly resisted, such pressure can be a serious hindrance to the development of a person's rightful gifts.

The kind of perception and kind of judgment people naturally prefer determine the direction in which they can develop most fully and effectively and with most personal satisfaction. When people use their two best-liked processes in a purposeful effort to do something well, their skill with those processes increases. People may be tempted to try to do everything with these two alone, regardless of their appropriateness to the purpose.

The recognition that one process is more appropriate than another in a given situation is an important milestone in type development. Without that recognition, people have no conscious reason to care, or even notice, which process they are using. When people realize that sensing works better than intuition for gathering facts, but intuition is better for seeing possibilities, or that thinking is better suited to organizing work, but feeling is better in human relations, they have the key to more effective use of *all their gifts*, each in its own field.

Full development of type involves getting to be expertly skilled with the dominant process, which actually bosses the other three processes and sets the major goals in life. Type development also depends on skilled use of the auxiliary process, which is vital for balance, because it supplies judgment if the dominant is perceptive or perception if the dominant is judging. Finally, full type development requires learning to use the two less-favored and less-developed processes appropriately.

The less-developed processes are always a problem. In managing them, it is useful to think of sensing, intuition, thinking, and feeling as four people living under one roof. The dominant process is head of the household, and the auxiliary is second in command. These two supplement each other, and neither encroaches on the other's domain; but in most situations, the two less-developed processes have a different view, based on the opposite kind of perception, and a different plan of action, coming from the opposite kind of judgment.

Dealing with the dissenters by denying them any hearing at all does not get rid of the problem, but merely imprisons processes of the mind, like slaves in a dungeon; if they are suppressed to that extent, they eventually break out and come up to consciousness in violent revolt. Because they were necessarily neglected while the preferred processes were developed, they are immature and cannot be expected to offer deep wisdom.

A person can, however, profitably accept them as younger members of the family, who are entitled to speak up in family councils before decisions are made. If they are given assignments that use their respective gifts and if their help is appreciated and their contributions seriously considered, they will, like children, grow steadily wiser, and the quality of their contributions will steadily improve.

Use of Perception

The accuracy of a decision—a judgment—can be no better than the accuracy of the information on which it rests. There is a time to perceive and a time to judge, and they occur in that order. In fact, the most sound decisions are based on both sensing and intuition.

Each kind of perception has its proper, indispensable uses. The greatest utility of sensing in practical matters lies in its awareness of the actual, existing situation and its grasp of the relevant facts. Respect for facts is the aspect of sensing most important for intuitives as well as sensing types to cultivate. Although naturally tending to be more interested in the possibilities than in the realities, intuitives can make a serious mistake by carrying their tendency to the point of overlooking the facts and the limitations the facts impose. Failure to accept and deal with the realities of a situation can make the intuitive's possibilities impossible.

Either perceptive process can be self-defeating if it becomes absolute, cutting off all help it needs from its opposite. Intuitives can bar help from sensing by assuming that there are no facts to be known on the point in question, or that they already know all the facts, or that the facts they don't know are not important.

Similarly, if sensing types assume that what they have already seen is all there is to see, they completely close off their intuition so it cannot contribute to their conscious thoughts. People who habitually make this assumption dislike the sudden and unexpected because their security rests on knowing from experience what to do. When something outside their experience threatens to happen, they can only give up and let it happen or else fight it blindly. Neither way of meeting the threat is productive, and both are stressful. It is far better to invite intuition to help *solve* the problem.

Use of Judgment

An essential skill to acquire is the ability to direct judgment where it is needed. Some people dislike the very idea of "judging," because they think it is authoritarian, restrictive, and arbitrary. This concept of judgment—a thing people use on each other—misses the main point. Judgment should be used on one's own concerns, for the better management of one's gifts, responsibilities, and life.

Some uses of judgment involve the individual only, such as the shaping of personal standards of conduct or the choosing of objectives. The latter covers a wide range, because the great satisfactions vary so much from type to type. An INTP once wrote, "For my type a search for truth is the most important thing. I have even surprised myself at the extent to which I will sacrifice personal comfort and happiness to arrive at understanding." For ISTJs, the major satisfaction might be the trust and respect of their community for their long records of unfailing public service and integrity. For INFPs, intent on possibilities for people, the major satisfaction might be in communicating an understanding that can help other people. For EFJ types, probably the major satisfaction lies in fellowship and personal relationships.

Most decisions, however, involve a present situation that needs either logic (thinking) or tact (feeling). People naturally tend to base decisions on the preferred kind of judgment, without considering its suitability. This is a mistake. If the merits of each kind of judgment are understood, thinkers can use feeling to gain cooperation, and feeling types can use thinking to take a careful look at the consequences.

If thinking is the more-trusted, it will resist being shut off, even temporarily, to give feeling the right of way. The resistance can be overcome if it is clear that feeling is contributing *only in the service of thinking.* The thinker's logic is based on facts, and feelings are facts. Because other people's feelings cause unexpected complications, thinkers need to count their own feelings among important causes and other people's feelings among important effects. Whenever other people are involved, a thinker's logic will be more accurate and successful if it gets help from feeling.

Similarly, if feeling is the more-trusted kind of judgment, it will resist challenges to its values from thinking, but a temporary shut-off can be tolerated on the understanding that thinking is being consulted *only in the service of feeling.* Cherished feeling values can be better served if thinking is given a chance to anticipate possible unfortunate consequences of an intended act.

Solving Problems in a Group

In a group activity that includes a variety of types, it is easy to see that each process contributes to the joint undertaking. For example, sensing types are likely to have precise information about the situation and to remember facts that others may have forgotten or overlooked, whereas intuitives are full of ways to circumvent any difficulties and often propose new procedures. Thinking types tend to be skeptical on principle and quick to challenge unfounded assumptions, to foresee what may go wrong, to point out flaws and inconsistencies in the plan, and to bring people back to the point when they stray. Feeling types are concerned with harmony; when sharp differences of opinion arise, they seek a compromise that preserves for each type (including their own) the features of most value to that type.

If the group is composed of very different types, agreement will be harder to reach than if the group was heterogeneous, but the decision will be far more broadly based and thoroughly considered, and thus in less danger of turning out badly for an unforeseen reason.

Using Problems to Develop Skills

The ability to use perception and judgment appropriately is a skill that can be acquired by practice, and life supplies much to practice on. When confronted by a problem to solve, a decision to make, or a situation to deal with, try exercising one process at a time, consciously and purposefully, each in its own field, without interference from other processes, and in the following order:

- *Sensing* to face the facts, to be realistic, to find exactly what the situation is and what is being done about it. Sensing can help you avoid wishful thinking or sentiment that may obscure the realities. To activate your sensing process, consider how the situation would look to a wise, impartial bystander.

- *Intuition* to discover all the possibilities—all the ways in which you might change the situation, your approach, or other people's attitudes. Try to put aside your natural assumption that you have been doing the obviously right thing.

- *Thinking* to impersonally analyze cause and effect, including all the consequences of the alternative solutions, pleasant and unpleasant, those that weigh for and those that weigh against your preferred solution. Consider the full costs involved and examine misgivings you may have suppressed because of loyalty to someone, liking for something, or reluctance to change your stand.

- *Feeling* to weigh how deeply you care about the things that will be gained or lost by each of the alternatives. In making a fresh appraisal, try not to let the temporary outweigh the permanent, however agreeable or disagreeable the immediate prospect may be. Consider as well other people's feelings, reasonable and unreasonable, about the various outcomes, and include your feelings and theirs among the facts to be considering in deciding which solution will work best.

The final decision will have sounder basis than usual, because of your consideration of facts, possibilities, consequences, and human values.

Some steps in this exercise are easier than others. The ones that use your best processes are fun. The others can be difficult at first, because they call for the strengths of types very different from yours, and those are strengths in which you have had relatively little practice. When the problem is important, you may wish to consult someone to whom those strengths come naturally, because he or she may have a strikingly different view of the situation and can help you to understand and use the neglected opposite side of yourself.

Learning to use your less-liked processes when they are needed is worth all the effort it takes. They not only contribute to a better solution of the present problem, but also prepare you to handle subsequent problems with more skill.

Using Type in Career Choice

Knowing which kinds of perception and judgment people prefer can help them choose a career. Of course, people want interesting and enjoyable work, so they want a career that calls for their best kinds of perception and judgment, but does not require much use of the opposite processes.

A good way to begin the search for a career is to look at the occupations that appeal most to people whose best-liked perception and judgment are the same as yours (see Chapter 14). Do not discount other fields; if you are attracted to a field that is unpopular with your type, you may prove to be valuable there as a supplier of complementary abilities and as a champion of changes that need to be made. Keep in mind, however, that if most of the people in that occupation are opposite to you in both perceptive and judging processes, they are unlikely to lend you much support; you will need to understand their types and carefully communicate when you need their cooperation.

Outer and Inner Worlds

Having found a field of interest where you can use your best skills, consider whether you prefer to work in the outer world of people and things or in the inner world of concepts and ideas. Although you live in both worlds, certainly you are more at home in one of the worlds and there you can do your best work.

If you are an extravert, find out whether the work you are considering has enough action or interaction with people to keep you interested. If you are an introvert, consider whether the work will give you enough chance to concentrate on what you are doing.

Judging and Perceptive Processes in the Outer World

Your preference between judging and perception determines the last letter of your type. J people rely mainly on judging for dealing with people and situations. Wanting to regulate and control life, they live in a planned and orderly way. P people, tending to rely on a perceptive process, live in a flexible, spontaneous way, and want to understand life and adapt to it.

If you are a judging type, find out if the work you are considering is reasonably predictable and organized or has to be played by ear from hour to hour. If you are a perceptive type, find out roughly how many decisions you will be expected to make in a day.

Using Type in Human Relations

Two people who prefer the same kinds of perception and judgment have the best chance of understanding each other and feeling understood. They look at things in much the same way and come to similar conclusions. They find the same things interesting and consider the same things important. Two people, alike in their kind of perception or their kind of judgment but not both, have the makings of a good working relationship. Their shared preference gives them common ground and their dissimilar preference gives them, as a team, a wider range of expertness than either has alone.

When co-workers differ on both perception and judgment, they have a problem. Working together will teach them something valuable if they respect each other, but it can be disastrous if they do not. As a team, they have at their disposal skill in both kinds of perception and both kinds of judgment. They need to understand each other well enough to see the merit of the other's skills and to use them.

If a husband and wife differ in this way, they may have an excellent marriage, but only if each appreciates and takes delight in the other's strengths. Because marriage is probably the most human of all human relationships, it has a whole chapter of its own (see Chapter 11).

Any relationship will suffer if oppositeness on a preference is treated as an inferiority. The parent-child relationship suffers severely if parents try to make their children into copies of themselves. Children have difficulty in dealing with a parent's wish that they were something that they definitely are not. Children who are feeling types may try to falsify their type and young thinking types may resist with hostility, but neither reaction can repair the damage to their faith in themselves. After taking the Type Indicator, many adults with such a childhood behind them have said, "What a relief to be told that it's all right to be the kind of person I am!"

Using Type in Communication

People with opposite preferences grow up side by side with practically no idea of how to communicate effectively with each other. Thinkers communicate in a thinking fashion and feeling types in a feeling fashion; this works when they communicate with their own type. However, when they need agreement or cooperation from their opposites, it does not work well.

Thinkers are by nature impersonal and critical of anything they consider wrong. They arrive by logic at definite opinions about what should be done differently, and they do not pay much attention to feelings, their own or other people's. When they disagree with feeling types, thinkers may state their disagreement so forcefully and bluntly that the feeling types feel attacked; this makes agreement or cooperation impossible.

Communication with feeling types should *make use of their feeling*. They prize harmony, and if given a chance, they would rather agree than not. When thinkers need to criticize a proposal or disagree with what has been done, they should start by mentioning the points on which they do agree. When assured that the thinkers are in the same camp with them, the feeling types are ready to make concessions to preserve the harmony and stay in the same camp. Then the points of disagreement can be discussed rather than fought over, and the thinkers' logic and the feeling types' understanding of people can both be brought to bear on the problem.

Communication with a thinker should be as logical and orderly as the feeling type can make it. Feeling types should be careful not to ignore facts and reasons that thinkers have already given. Although feeling types speak from a strong belief in the value of what they advocate, they must respect the thinkers' estimate of the costs of the consequences.

If you are a feeling type, remember that thinkers rely on reasoning from cause to effect but usually do not know how other people feel about things until they are told. Therefore, let them know, briefly and cheerfully, how you feel about things so that they can include your feelings among the causes from which they can expect effects.

Communication between sensing and intuitive types often breaks down before it gets started. If you are the intuitive, you need to observe the following rules: First, say explicitly, *at the start*, what you are talking about. (Otherwise, you are requiring your sensing listeners to hold what you say in mind until they can figure out what you are referring to, which they seldom think is worth doing.) Second, finish your sentences; you know what the rest of the sentence is, but your listeners do not. Third, give notice when changing the subject. And last, don't switch back and forth between subjects. Your listeners cannot see the parentheses. Finish one point and move *explicitly* to the next.

If you are the sensing type, the intuitive's words may seem to ignore or even contradict facts you know to be true, but don't ignore what was said or dismiss it as foolish. It may contain an idea that could be useful, and your facts should be useful to the author of the idea. The constructive course is to state your facts as a contribution to the subject, *not as a refutation of the idea*. Progress in almost any direction needs contributions from both sides, facts from the sensing type and unfamiliar ideas from the intuitive.

The most successful compromises preserve the advantages that each type considers most important. People often make an all-out effort for a scheme as a whole, when what they truly care about is a particular merit that could be incorporated into another plan. Sensing types want the solution to be workable, thinkers want it systematic, feeling types want it humanly agreeable, and intuitives want a door left open for growth and improvement. These are all reasonable desires. Given understanding and good will, they should be achievable.

When people differ, a knowledge of type lessens friction and eases strain. In addition, it reveals the *value of differences*. No one has to be good at everything. By developing individual strengths, guarding against known weaknesses, and appreciating the strengths of the other types, life will be more amusing, more interesting, and more of a daily adventure than it could possibly be if everyone were alike.

Looking to the Future

I have looked at the world from the standpoint of type for more than fifty years and have found the experience constantly rewarding. An understanding of type can be rewarding for society, too. It is not too much to hope that wider and deeper understanding of the gifts of diversity may eventually reduce the misuse and nonuse of those gifts. It should lessen the waste of potential, the loss of opportunity, and the number of dropouts and delinquents. It may even help with the prevention of mental illness.

Whatever the circumstances of your life, whatever your personal ties, work, and responsibilities, the understanding of type can make your perceptions clearer, your judgments sounder, and your life closer to your heart's desire.

> *For as we have many members in one body,*
>   *and all members have not the same office:*
> *So we, being many, are one body...*
>   *and every one members one of another.*
>
> *Having then gifts differing...*
>   *whether prophecy, let us prophesy...*
> *Or ministry, let us wait on our ministering:*
>   *or he that teacheth, on teaching;*
> *Or he that exhorteth, on exhortation....*

Rom. 12: 4–8

Endnotes

1   Van der Hoop (who includes the effects of the auxiliary in his descriptions of the types) makes this point explicitly. "The subsidiary function frequently tends to control adaptation in the direction towards which the dominant function is not oriented. For example, an introvert of thinking-type will employ his instinct [sensing] or his intuition particularly for purposes of external adjustment. Or an extraverted intuitive will seek contact with the inner world through thought or feeling." (1939, p. 93)

2   The revised translations of these quoted passages may be found in the Bolligen Series XX, Vol. 6 (Jung, 1971), pp. 405, 406, 387, and 340.

3   "Sensational" also has distracting connotations which have been avoided by use of the shorter form "sensing," and "process" has been used instead of "function," so that the mental processes of perception and judgment may be discussed at any level without the distraction of a less familiar term.

4   See Chapters 4–7, Figures 24–27.

5   Form D2 has been supplanted by Forms G and F; see Myers, 1962.

6   In an early, unpublished study by Isabel Briggs Myers, the Type Indicator was given to male students from eleventh and twelfth grades of a high school serving the whole city of Stamford, Connecticut. Introverts made up 28.1 percent of the 217 students in the eleventh grade and 25.8 percent of the 182 in twelfth grade.

7   Hence, the importance of firm, fair discipline in building a person's character from infancy on. At the start, the parents are the children's judgment. If parents waver, the children have nothing to judge by, but if parents set a consistent standard by which the young ones must measure their conduct and govern themselves, the parents give the priceless habit of judging one's own actions, years before the children are old enough to set up their own effective standards. Self-judgment is the beginning of character. Undisciplined children acquire it much later, more painfully, and less thoroughly, if at all.

8   In introverts these characteristics are somewhat modified by the perceptive nature of the dominant process

9   In introverts these characteristics are somewhat modified by the judging nature of the dominant process.

10 An introverted sensing type said about an extraverted admirer: "He complains that when we are together he does all the talking. Really, it is a two-way conversation—what he says to me and what I say to me. Only what I say isn't out loud."

11 This incident is from the author's unpublished personal research at First Pennsylvania Bank (Philadelphia). Frequency ratio is from Chapter 3, Figures 6 and 7, showing data gathered by author and processed by Educational Testing Service.

12 Author's unpublished research.

13 The Monograph entitled *Myers Longitudinal Medical Study*, which describes both follow-up studies, may be obtained from the Center for Applications of Psychological Type, 1441 Northwest 6th Street, Suite B-400, Gainesville, Florida 32601.

14 The total drop-out rate from medical school is somewhat higher than these percentages would indicate. The known permanent drop-outs from this sample included neither those students who dropped out before their class took the Type Indicator, nor those who dropped out temporarily and later were admitted to and graduated from another school.

15 The last letter of the type formula, J or P, shows whether the outer world is dealt with in the judging or the perceptive attitude. In extraverts the last letter describes the General; in introverts it describes the Aide. The first letter, E or I, always describes the General.

16 An early, unpublished study by Isabel Briggs Myers is the basis of statements in this chapter about the frequencies of types in the general population. The Type Indicator was given to male students from the eleventh and twelfth grades of a high school serving the whole city of Stamford, Connecticut. Among the 217 students in the eleventh grade, 28.1 percent were introverts and 26.7 percent were intuitives; among the 182 twelfth-graders, 25.8 percent were introverts and 33.0 were intuitives. The percent of intuitives may have increased because of sensing types leaving school after their attendance was no longer compulsory.

References

Bogart, D. R. (1975). *Myers-Briggs Type Indicator preferences as a differentiating factor in skill acquisition during short-term counseling training*. Unpublished paper.

Briggs, K. C. Unpublished research.

Bruner, J. S. (1960). *The process of education*. Cambridge, MA: Harvard University Press.

Grant, W. H. (1965). *Behavior of MBTI types* (Research report). Auburn, AL: Auburn University Student Counseling Service.

Gray, H., & Wheelwright, J. B. (1944). Jung's psychological types and marriage. *Stanford Medical Bulletin 2*, 37–39.

Gundlach, R. H., & Gerum, E. (1931). Vocational interests and types of ability. *Journal of Educational Psychology, 22*, 505.

Hay, E. N. Personal communication, 1943–1946.

Hebb, D. 0. (1949). *The organization of intelligence*. New York: Wiley.

Hunt, J. M. (1961). *Intelligence and experience*. New York: Ronald Press.

Jacobi, J. (1968). *The psychology of C. G. Jung*. New Haven, CT: Yale University Press.

Jung, C. G. (1923). *Psychological types*. New York: Harcourt Brace.

Jung, C. G. (1971). *Psychological types*. Bollingen Series XX. The Collected Works of C. G. Jung (Vol. 6). Princeton, NJ: Princeton University Press.

Kanner, J. (1975). Personal communication.

Laney, A. R. (1946–1950). Personal communication.

Laney, A. R. (1949). *Occupational implications of the Jungian personality function-types as identified by the Briggs-Myers Type Indicator*. Unpublished master's thesis, George Washington University, Washington, DC.

MacKinnon, D. W. (1961). *The personality correlates of creativity: A study of American architects*. Berkeley, CA: Institute of Personality Assessment and Research.

MacKinnon, D. W. (1962). Personal communication.

McCaulley, M. H. (1977). *The Myers longitudinal medical study (Monograph II)*. Gainesville, FL: Center for Applications of Psychological Type.

McCaulley, M. H. (1978). *Application of the Myers-Briggs Type Indicator to medicine and other health professions (Monograph I)*. Gainesville, FL: Center for Applications of Psychological Type.

Miller, P. V. (1965). *The contribution of noncognitive variables to the prediction of student performance in law school*. Unpublished doctoral discertation, University of Pennsylvania.

Miller, P. V. (1967). *The contribution of noncognitive variables to the prediction of student performance in law school*. Follow-up study, University of Pennsylvania.

Myers, I. B. (1962). *The Myers-Briggs Type Indicator*. Palo Alto, CA: Consulting Psychologists Press.

Myers, I. B. (1976). *Introduction to type* (rev. ed.). Palo Alto, CA: Consulting Psychologists Press.

Myers, I. B. Unpublished research.

Myers, I. B., & Davis, J. A. *Relation of medical students' psychological type to their specialties twelve years later* (ETS RM 64–15). Princeton, NJ: Educational Testing Service.

Nippon Recruit Center. (1977). *Report on Japanese translation and examination of MBTI*. Tokyo: Nippon Recruit Center.

Piaget, J. (1936). *Origins of intelligence in children*. New York: International Universities Press.

Pines, M. (1966). *Revolution in learning*. New York: Harper & Row.

Plattner, P. (1950). *Glücklichere ehen: Prakzische ehepsychologie*. Bern: H. Huber.

Rowe, M. B. (1974). Pausing phenomena: Influence on the quality of instruction. *Journal of Psycholinguistic Research, 3*, 203–224.

Rowe, M. B. (1974). Wait-time and rewards as instructional variables, their influence on language, logic, and fate control. Part 1: Wait-time. *Journal of Research in Science Teaching,11*, 81–94.

Spranger, E. (1928). *Types of men*. Halle, E. Germany: Niemeyer.

Stephens, W. B. (1972). *Relationship between selected personality characteristics of senior art students and their area of art study*. Unpublished doctoral dissertation, University of Florida, Gainesville.

Thurstone, L. L. (1931). A multiple factor study of vocational interests. *Personnel Journal, 10*, 198–205.

Van der Hoop, J. H. (1939). *Conscious orientation*. New York: Harcourt Brace.

Vernon, P. E. (1938). The assessment of psychological qualities by verbal methods. *Industrial Health Research Board Reports, No. 83*. London: H. M. Statistical Office.

von Fange, E. A. (1961). *Implications for school administration of the personality structure of educational personnel*. Unpublished doctoral dissertation, University of Alberta, Alberta, Canada.

		SENSING TYPES	
		With Thinking	**With Feeling**
INTROVERTS	**Judging**	**ISTJ** Introverted Sensing with thinking	**ISFJ** Introverted Sensing with feeling
	Perceptive	**ISTP** Introverted Thinking with sensing	**ISFP** Introverted Feeling with sensing
EXTRAVERTS	**Perceptive**	**ESTP** Extraverted Sensing with thinking	**ESFP** Extraverted Sensing with feeling
	Judging	**ESTJ** Extraverted Thinking with sensing	**ESFJ** Extraverted Feeling with sensing

INTUITIVE TYPES			
With Feeling	**With Thinking**		
INFJ Introverted Intuition with feeling	**INTJ** Introverted Intuition with thinking	Judging	INTROVERTS
INFP Introverted Feeling with intuition	**INTP** Introverted Thinking with intuition	Perceptive	
ENFP Extraverted Intuition with feeling	**ENTP** Extraverted Intuition with thinking	Perceptive	EXTRAVERTS
ENFJ Extraverted Feeling with intuition	**ENTJ** Extraverted Thinking with intuition	Judging	

Index

Academics and type, 44–46, 158. *See also* Type(s), incidences of among
Auxiliary process
  balance of, 11–12, 19–21, 174, 193
    inadequate, 176–177
    for introverts vs. extraverts, 19–21
  Briggs' interpretation of, 22
  described, 11–12
  dominant vs., 11, 18, 90
  Jung's
    minimally treated, 17–18
    theoretical extension of, 18
  types and, 21, 83
    extraverted sensing, 101
    extraverted thinking, 86–87
    introverted intuition, 110
    introverted thinking, 89
  underdevelopment of, 84
  See also Dominant process; Processes
AVL Study of Values, 159

Balance. *See* Auxiliary process, balance provided by
Bogart, D. R., on type and counseling training, 152
Briggs, Katharine C.
  Myers-Briggs Type Indicator Manual, 31, 41

views on
  extraverted vs. introverted processes, 77
  personality types, 22
  See also Myers, I. B.
Bruner, J. S., on early learning, 133

Careers. *See* Occupation(s)
Children
  excellence in, Jung on, 188
  intelligence of, 133
  learning in, 133–138
    communication, 139–145
    defenses against, 187–188
    failure and, 187
    interest in, 145–147
    language, 59, 135–136
    reading, 140–142
    responsibility and, 187
    satisfaction earned and, 185–187, 188–189
    sensing, 60–61, 135–136, 139–140, 145, 146
    styles of, 61, 108, 139, 143–147, 167
  type development in, 168–169, 170–171, 173, 181, 182–183, 185
    inadequate, 187–188
    introversion, 182–183

intuition, 61, 108, 135–136, 139, 145
judgment, 185–186, 187, 188
maturity and, 170–171, 175, 185
motivation for, 185–189
perceiving, 2–3, 183
sensing, scholastic interest of, 58–59, 60
Type Indicator for, 169
unconscious of, 131–132, 133, 134, 135
See also Education and teaching
Cognition, 1, 191. *See also* Children, learning in; Education and teaching; Intelligence; Judging process; Perceiving process
Communication. *See under* Interpersonal relations
Conflict. *See under* Interpersonal relations
Consciousness. *See* Unconscious
Crossover, 120–121, 129–130

Darwin, Charles Robert, extraversion of, 56
Dominant process
described, 9–11
determining, 14
development of, 84, 175, 193
Jung on, 11
medical school drop-outs related to, 159
opposition and, 11
sovereignty of, 11
of types, 15
EP (SN preference), 61–63
extraverted feeling, 93
extraverted intuition, 106
extraverted sensing, 99, 101
extraverted thinking, 86
introverted feeling, 96
introverted sensing, 102

introverted thinking, 89
introverts vs. extraverts, 12–14, 15, 22, 175
types as product of, 83
See also Auxiliary process; Processes
DOR. *See* Dropout Ratio
Drop-out rate and type, among law and medical students, 158–160. *See also* Type(s), incidences among
Dropout Ratio (DOR)
among law students, 49
described, 48–49
lowest, 94, 104

Education and teaching
application vs. interest, 146–147
appropriate to type, 61, 145–146, 167, 171, 188
principles for, 136–138
reading, 142
testing, 143–145
time and type, 144–145
See also Children, learning in; Occupation(s), kind of, teaching
Educational Testing Service, 142
EFJ types, described, 195
EF types, occupation for, 158
Einstein, Albert, introversion of, 56, 89
EI preference
auxiliary process in, 20–21, 84
described, 7
development of, 170, 174
effect of, 53–55
independence of, 7, 57
occupations and, 152, 153
opposites in, 23, 125
marital partners, 125
work reactions of, 154

traits of, 56
Type Table division of, 28
ENFJ type
  described, 95
  incidences of in various populations, 31–51
  medical specialties preferred by, 160–161
  traits of, 92, 98
ENFP type
  described, 109
  example of, 128
  incidences of in various populations, 31–51
  medical specialties preferred by, 161
  traits of, 98, 105–106
ENP types, occupation for, 158
ENTJ type
  described, 88
  incidences of in various populations, 31–51
  medical specialties of, 161
  occupation for, 85
  traits of, 85
ENTP type
  described, 108–109
  examples of, 55, 157
  marital partner preferences of, 126
  medical specialties preferred by, 161
  traits of, 105–106
EP types
  development of, 178–179
  of SN preference, 63
ESFJ type
  described, 94–95
  incidences of in various populations, 31–51, 182
  medical specialties preferred by, 160–161
  SSRs of among students, 45
  traits of, 92

weakness, 156
ESFP type
  described, 101–102
  example of, 156
  incidences of in various populations, 31–51
  medical specialties preferred by, 161–162
  traits of, 99
ESF types, weakness of, 117
ESTJ type
  described, 87
  drop-out rate of among medical students, 160
  incidence(s) of
    among students, 33
    in various populations, 31–51, 182
  marital partner preferences of, 126
  medical specialties preferred by, 161–162
  occupations for, 85, 149, 152, 159, 160, 162
  traits of, 85
  sex differences, 87
ESTP type
  described, 101
  incidences of in various populations, 31–51
  medical specialties preferred by, 161–162
  traits of, 99
ES types
  examples of, 100, 158
  occupations for, 30
  ESTs, 7, 152
  SSRs of among students, 42
  traits of
    learning style, 141–142
    weakness, 173
E types. *See* Extravert types
Extraversion process
  defined, 7

dominant vs. auxiliary in, 12–14,
15, 19–21, 22, 175
Jung's minimal treatment of auxiliary in, 19–21
SN preference and, 57
in Western civilization, extent of,
54, 182
See also EI preference; Extravert
types
Extravert types
described, 53–55
examples of, 7, 55, 56
introvert vs.
among students, 159
conflict between, 123
development of, 168–169
occupations for, 54–55,
152–153, 154, 156, 160, 163,
198
population occurrences of, 182
processes of, 79–81
similarities between, 83–84
JP auxiliary process of, 73, 176
judging preferred by, 86, 93
marital partner preferences of,
124–125
SSRs of among students, 46
traits of, 56
See also EI preference; Extraversion process; individually listed
(letter-designated) extravert
types

Feeling process
appropriate use of, 178, 179, 195,
196, 197
as auxiliary in introverted intuitive, 110
defined, 3
EI preference and, 53
as dominant in extraverted
sensing, 99
for intuitives, 107

emotions vs., 192
opposition (thinking) to, 118–120,
127–130
See also Feeling types; Judging
process; Processes; TF
preference
Feeling types
described, 65, 120, 128, 169, 192,
193
extraverted, 92–94, 169
incidence of
among females, 34, 38, 66
among medical students, 159
introverted, 95–97
marriage of
shadow's effect on, 128, 130
to thinkers, 128–130
occupations for, 66, 150, 151, 154,
157, 161
SSRs of among students, 45, 48
thinking of, 66
traits of, 65–66, 68, 71, 122
communication style, 164, 200
sex differences, 34, 66. 182
See also Feeling process; individually listed (letter-designated)
feeling types; TF preferences
FJ types
law school success of, 158
marital partner preferences of,
124–125
traits of, 71
Ford, Henry, introverted thinking of,
89
FP types
law school success of, 158
Freud, Sigmund, extraversion of, 56
F types. *See* Feeling types

Grant, W. Harold, on type and occupation, 94, 149
Gray, H and Wheelwright, J. G., on
complementary mating, 123

Gundlach, R. H. and Gerum, E., on personality classifications, 6

Hebb, D. O., on early learning, 133
Human interaction. *See* Interpersonal relations
Hunt, J. M., on early learning, 133

IF types, medical careers for, 159
Indicator Manual, 160
INFJ type
    described, 112
    incidence(s) of
        among students, 33
        in various populations, 31–51
    medical specialties preferred by, 161
    traits of, 109
        communication tendency, 98
        intelligence, 66
INFP type
    auxiliary process balance in, 20
    described, 98, 195
    incidences of in various populations, 31–51
    medical school entrance rate of, 159
    medical specialties preferred by, 161–162
    traits of, 95–96
        intelligence, 66
Intelligence
    in children, 133
    Otis vs. Wechsler measures, 143
    testing of and type, 59–60, 66, 143
    type and, 59
        development as IQ substitute, 177
        for INs, 43, 66
Interpersonal relations
    communication
        with children, 136, 139
        co-workers', 94–95, 116, 163–164
        in marriage, 127–128
        problem-solving, 163, 196–197
        sensing vs. intuitive, 164, 200–201
        shadow's effect on, 128
        thinking vs. feeling, 3, 65–66, 86–87, 89, 91, 118–120, 128–130, 164, 200
        type and, 116–118, 164
    conflict
        crossover, 120–121, 129–130
        in marriage, 128–130, 164
        of opposites, 4, 115, 116, 123, 130, 163, 199
        See also Marriage
INTJ type
    described, 111–112
    incidences of in various populations, 31–51
    medical specialties preferred by, 161–162
    traits of, 109
INTP type
    described, 90–92
    examples of, 91, 157–158, 195
    incidences of in various populations, 31–51
    medical specialties of, 161–162
    occupations for, 157–158
    traits of, 88
Introversion process
    criticism of, 83
    defined, 7
    dominant vs. auxiliary, 11–14, 15, 19–21, 22, 83, 90, 175
        Briggs' interpretation of, 22
        hidden dominant process, 13–14, 20, 22, 175
        inadequate auxiliary, 177
Jung's
    archetypes and, 53

minimal treatment of auxiliary,
17–18, 19–21
See also EI preference; Introvert
types
Introvert types
advantages of, 54–55
children's learning and, 182–183
described, 53–55
examples of, 7, 53, 56, 73, 89
extravert vs.
among medical students, 159
conflict between, 123
development of, 168–169
occupations for, 54–55,
152–153, 154, 156, 160, 163,
198
population occurrences of, 182
processes of, 79–81
shadow's effect on, 84–85
similarities between, 83–84
incidences of among students, 38,
39
intuitive, 182
JP preference dominant for, 73
marital partner preferences of,
124–125
SSRs of among students, 46
traits of, 56
See also EI preference; individually
listed (letter-designated)
introvert types; Introversion
process
Intuition process
appropriate use of, 178, 197
defined, 2, 192
as dominant in extraverted
sensing, 99
EI preference and, 53
unconscious and, 2, 57, 59, 131
opposition (sensing) to, 120–122
See also Intuitive types;
Perceiving process; Processes;
SN preference

Intuitive types
described, 57–58, 169
education and, relation between,
34, 58, 131
extraverted, 105–108
incidence of
among college prep females, 38,
39
among college prep vs. nonprep
males, 32
among high school males, 33
among medical students, 159
among National Merit
Finalists, 37, 58
in various populations, 58, 182
introverted, 109–111
occupations for, 6, 61, 149, 150,
152, 153, 155, 157, 158, 161,
192
INs, 30, 66
SSRs of among students, 48
traits of, 62, 121, 192
communication style, 164,
200–201
intelligence and testing, 43, 59,
142–143
learning style, 61, 108,
135–136, 139, 145
weaknesses, 91, 92, 107–108,
194–195
See also individually listed (letter-
designated) intuitive types;
Intuition process; SN
preference
IN types
occupation for, 158
SSRs of
among engineering students, 41
among fine arts students, 44
among science students, 43
traits of, 43, 66
learning style of, 141

ISFJ type
    described, 104–105
    examples of, 85, 143
    incidence(s) of
        among National Merit
            finalists, 39
        in various populations, 31–51
    medical specialties preferred by,
        161
    occupations for, 61
    traits of, 102
        learning style, 59
ISFP type
    described, 97–98
    example of, 156
    incidences of in various popula-
        tions, 31–51
    medical specialties preferred by,
        160–161
    traits of, 95–96
ISTJ type
    auxiliary process balance in, 20
    described, 103–104, 195
    example of, 127, 156
    incidence(s) of
        among National Merit final-
            ists, 37
        in various populations, 31–51
    medical specialties preferred by,
        161
    SSRs of among students, 41
    traits of, 102
        learning style, 59–60
        sex differences, 104
ISTP type
    described, 90
    incidences of in various popula-
        tions, 31–51
    medical specialties preferred by,
        160–161
    traits of, 88
IST types, occupations for, 7, 152
I types. *See* Introvert types

Jacobi, Jolande, on thinking, 65
JP preference
    auxiliary process in, 20, 84
    Briggs' interpretation of, 22
    described, 8
    development of, 167, 170–171, 174
    dominant process in, 11, 14
    effect of, 69–74
    Jung's rational/irrational vs.,
        21–22
    occupations and, 150, 153,
        198–199
    opposites in, 8, 22, 23
        marital partners, 126
        work reactions of, 155
    Type Table division of, 28–29
J types. *See* Judging types
Jobs. *See* Occupation(s)
Judging process
    appropriate use of, 65, 86, 105,
        115, 195
    defined, 1
    opposition (perceiving) to, 8
    processes (feeling and thinking)
        of, 3, 65
    of types
        extraverted sensing, 101, 102
        extraverted thinking, 86
        introverts, 73
        intuitive, 107–108, 110
    See also Feeling process; JP
        preference; Judging types;
        Thinking process
Judging types
    described, 69–71, 167, 195
    development of, 176–177,
        178–179, 185
    drop-out rate of among students,
        158–160
    examples of, 8, 191
    extraverted, 86, 93
    incidence of among students, 35
    occupations and, 153, 155

perception of, inadequate, 70, 176
SSRs of among school administrators, 51, 71
traits of, 69, 70–71, 75
   learning style of, 146–147
See also individually listed (letter-
   designated) judging types; JP
   preference; Judging process
Jung, Carl G.
   introversion of, 7, 56, 89
   shadow theory of, 84–85, 128, 130
   type theory of, 17–24
      applied, 24
      archetypes, 53
      auxiliary process, 17–18,
         19–20
      criticism of, 83
      opposites, 23–24
      original types, 30
      preference effects on personal-
         ity, 24
   views of about
      dominant process, 11
      excellence in children, 188
      extraverted intuitives, 106
      extraverted thinkers, 86
      extravert-introvert conflict,
         123
      feeling as rational, 192
      introverts, 55
      marriage and type, 123
      process development, 175
      rational vs. irrational, 21–22
      type falsification, 181
      ways of perceiving, 2
      See also Psychological Types;
         Type(s)

Kanner, Joseph, on Otis vs. Wechsler
   measures, 143
Kant, Immanuel, introverted
   thinking of, 89

Laney, A. R., on types and occupation, 151, 153, 157
Lincoln, Abraham, introversion of,
   56

MacKinnon, D. W., on type and
   occupation, 149
McCaulley, M. H., on type and
   occupation, 94, 159
Marriage
   complementary mating in, 123
   conflict in, 128–129, 164
   Jung on type and, 123–124
   preferences in, 123–127
   traits of good, 127
   type and, 123–130, 199
   See also Interpersonal relations
Miller, P. V., on type and education,
   158
Myers, I. B.
   on type and occupation, 151, 153,
      159
   Myers-Briggs Indicator Manual,
      31, 41
   See also Briggs, Katharine C.

NF types
   occupations for, 151–152, 158
   SSRs of
      among art students, 46
      among counseling students, 47
      among liberal arts students, 40
   traits of, 98, 117
Nippon Recruit Center, 158
NTP type, example of, 128
NT types, occupations for, 152
N types. *See* Intuition types

Occupation(s)
   kind of
      accounting, 103, 150, 151, 157
      art, 98, 109, 152, 158

banking, 150, 151, 156, 157, 158
business, 7, 152, 159
   executive, 85, 88, 91, 103, 107, 108, 110
construction, 150
counseling, 30, 66, 95, 98, 107, 108, 109, 151, 158, 160
crafts, 97, 105
customer relations, 112, 150, 151
economics, 7, 90, 152
engineering, 30, 100, 110, 111
finance, 30, 150, 152
forecasting, 152
invention, 108, 111, 152
law, 7, 67, 103, 150, 152, 158
literature, 98, 107, 158
machinery, 100, 192
mathematics, 90, 112
medicine, 67, 94, 97, 104, 150–151, 159–160
   specialties by type, 160–162
military, 100, 104–105, 110
ministry, 95, 98, 152
politics, 107
production, 150
promotion, 108
research, 91, 98, 111, 151, 152, 160
sales, 66, 109, 150, 151
science, 90, 98, 108, 109, 110, 111, 150, 151, 152
service, 94, 149, 150
statistics, 90
teaching, 91, 95, 98, 107, 108, 109, 150–151, 152
technical, 66, 103, 158
transcription, 103–104, 156
trouble-shooting, 108
for types
   ES, 30

extraverts vs. introverts, 54–55, 152–153, 154, 156, 160, 163, 198
feeling, 5, 66, 153
intuitive, 6, 61, 149, 150, 152, 153, 157, 158, 160, 161, 192
INs, 30, 66
JP, 150, 153, 198–199
sensing, 5, 61, 149, 150, 153, 155, 158, 161, 162, 163
thinking, 30, 67, 150, 153, 192
type's use in
   career choice, 159, 198–199
      against type, 152
      preferences' influence on, 150, 153–156
   incidences of types in jobs, 151
   job satisfaction, 116, 153, 156–158, 163–164
   multicultural application, 158
   turnover, 153
   See also Self-selection ratio (SSR); Type(s), incidences of among
Opposites
   appropriate use of, 118, 119, 174–175, 178, 199
   conflict of, 4, 115, 116, 123, 130, 163, 199
   crossover, 118, 120–121, 129–130
   dominant process and, 11
   feeling vs. thinking, 23, 118–120, 127–130
   intuitive vs. sensing, 120–122
   in marriage, 23, 125–126, 130
   in preferences, 8, 22–23, 125
   type and, 27, 119
   at work, 153–156
Otis test, 143

Perceiving process
   appropriate use of, 86, 105, 115–116, 194

defined, 1
processes (intuition and
     sensing) of, 2, 57
opposition (judging) to, 8
of types
     extraverted feeling, 93
     extraverted intuitive, 106
     extraverted sensing, 101
     extraverted thinking, 86–87
     introverts, 73, 89
See also Intuition process; JP
     preference; Perceiving types;
     Sensing process
Perceiving types
among medical students, 159
described, 69–70, 71–73, 167, 194
examples of, 8, 69, 70, 73, 191
judgment as auxiliary in, 70, 176,
     178
occupations for, 153, 155,
     198–199
traits of, 69–70, 71–73, 75
See also individually listed (letter-
     designated) perceiving types; JP
     preference; Perceiving process
Personality
classification systems of, 6
dominant process on, effect of, 10
neurosis and type development,
     181
preferences' effect on, 4
See also Theories; Type(s), devel-
     opment
Piaget, J., on children's intelligence,
     133, 135, 137
Pines, Maya, on early learning, 133,
     135
Plattner, P., on extravert-introvert
     marriages, 123
Practical applications of type, 24. *See
     also* Education and teaching;
     Interpersonal relations;
     Marriage; Occupation(s)

Preferences
combined, 4
     job satisfaction and, 116,
          153–158, 163–164
     Jung's minimal treatment of,
          17, 19
     described, 5–6
     pairs, 22
     as type, 9, 77, 83
     Type Table location and
          changes, 28, 29, 51, 55
     uniqueness through interaction
          of, 4, 30, 77
     "with" and dominance, 30
development of, 2, 3, 9, 20, 170
effects of, 9
     on marital choice, 123–127
inborn, 8, 167, 168, 193
independence of, 4, 7, 57
in marriages, 124, 126
occupations and, 150, 159
summarized, 8–9
See also EI preference; JP prefer-
     ence; SN preference;
     TF preference; Type(s)
Processes
co-existence of, 194
development of, 193–194, 198;
     ISTJs' third, 104
dominance of one, 11
inborn, 193
order of, importance of, 163, 197
preferred, 77
See also Auxiliary process;
     Dominant process; Feeling
     process; Intuition process;
     Sensing process; Thinking
     process
Psychological Types, 17, 22, 77
auxiliary process, 18
dominant process, 11
JPs, 19, 21
ways of perceiving, 2

See also Jung, Carl G.

P types. *See* Perceiving types

Roosevelt, Franklin Delano, extraversion of, 56
Rowe, Mary Budd, on children's learning, 144
Roosevelt, Theodore, extraversion of, 56

Self-selection ratio (SSR)
  among
    art education students, 46
    college science students, 43
    counselor education students, 47
    engineering students, 41
    finance/commerce students, 42
    fine arts students, 44
    law students, 49
    liberal arts students, 40
    police, 50
    Rhodes Scholars, 48
    school administrators, 51
  defined, 39
  highest, 104, 159
  See also Occupation(s)
Sensing process
  appropriate use of, 178, 197
  defined, 2, 57
  EI preference and, 53
  opposition (intuition) to, 120–122
  See also Perceiving process; Processes; Sensing types; SN preference
Sensing types
  described, 58, 60, 169, 192
  extent of
    in Britain, 58
    in Western civilization, 182
  extraverted
    described, 99–101
    learning style of, 100–101

  incidence of
    among high school females, 35, 39
    among high school males, 33, 37
    among police, 50
  introverted, 102–103
  occupations for, 5, 61, 149, 150, 153, 155, 158, 161, 162, 163
  traits of, 62, 121–122
    communication style, 164, 200–201
    intelligence and testing, 59–60, 143
    learning style, 59–61, 139–140, 145–146
  weakness of, 195
  See also individually listed (letter-designated) sensing types; Sensing process; SN preference
Sex differences and type, 34, 66, 87, 104, 182
SFP example of, 156–157
SF types, occupations for, 150–151
Shadow, described, 84–85, 128, 130
SN preference
  defined, 3, 57
  described, 57–61
  development of, 169, 170–171
  effect of, 57–61
  EP type in, 63
  example of, 146
  frequency among marriage partners, 124
  as introverts or extraverts, 57
  marital partner likeness on, 126
  occupations and, 150, 155
  traits of, 62
    independence, 4, 7, 57
  Type Table division of, 28
Spranger, E., on personality classifications, 6
SSR. *See* Self-selection ratio

Stephens, W. B., on type and
      academics, 44–46, 158
Strong Vocational Interest Blank, 159
ST types, occupations for, 150
S types. *See* Sensing types

Teaching. *See* Education and
      teaching
TF preference
   described, 3
   development of, 169, 170–171, 179
   effect of, 65–67
   EJ type in, 67
   identification of, 28
   occupation and, 150
   opposites in, 23
      marital partners, 125
      work reactions of, 154
   traits of, 68
      independence, 4, 7
      sex differences, 34, 66
   Type Table division of, 28
Theories
   complementary mating, 123
   type, 1
      Briggs', 22
      criticism of, 83
      excellence, 8
      unequal occurrences of, 182
      uniqueness, 1
   See also Jung, psychological types
      of
Thinking process
   appropriate use of, 178, 179,
      195–196, 197
   defined, 3
   as dominant in extraverted
      sensing, 99
   EI preference and, 53
   for intuitives, 107, 110
   quality of, 67
   opposition (feeling) to, 118–120,
      127–130

See also Judging process; Processes;
      TF preference; thinking types
Thinking types
   described, 65–67, 116, 128–129,
      169, 192
   extraverted, 85–87, 119
   incidence of
      among high school males, 38
      among males, 34, 38, 66
   introverted, 88–90
      auxiliary development of,
         89–90
      example of, 89
   marriage of to feeling types,
      128–130
   occupations for, 66, 150, 151, 154,
      157, 158, 161, 192
   SSRs of among students, 49
   traits of, 65, 67, 68, 122, 128
      communication style, 164, 200
      sex differences, 34, 66, 87, 104,
         182
      weaknesses, 128, 129–130
   See also individually listed (letter-
      designated) thinking types; TF
      preferences; Thinking process
Thurstone, L. L., on personality
      classifications, 6
TJ types
   law school success of, 158
   traits of, 71, 129
TP preference, DORs and SSRs of
      among students, 49
T types. *See* Thinking types
Type Indicator, 27, 73, 142, 156, 157,
      159, 199
   Japanese translation of, 158
   split-half reliability of, 169–170,
      171
Type(s)
   auxiliary process of, 21, 83
   Briggs', 22

children's learning styles and, 61, 139, 143–147, 167
creation of by preferences, 9, 77, 83
crossover, 120–121
culture and, 158
designations, 30
determining, 21, 23
development, 84, 116, 118, 167, 178
  appropriateness recognized, 193
  balanced, 11–12, 19–21, 174
  by problem-solving, 196–197
  good, 20, 173–174, 176, 181, 191, 193–194
    benefits of, 177, 201
  inadequate, 176–177, 181, 185–156, 194
  obstacles to, 181–183
  stages of, 168
differences
  appearance of, 181
  right to, 123, 130, 167, 301
dominant process of, 15, 83
inborn, 8, 167, 168, 193
incidences of among
  college students
    art, 46, 158
    counseling, 47, 151, 153
    education, 151
    engineering, 41
    finance/commerce, 42, 151
    fine arts, 44
    health-related, 151
    journalism, 151
    law, 49, 151, 158
    medicine, 161
    liberal arts, 40
    nursing, 151
    occupational therapy, 45
    science, 43, 151

  high school students
    college prep, 31, 33, 35, 36, 38
    females, 34, 35, 38, 39
    males, 31, 32, 33, 36, 37
    National Merit finalists, 37, 39
    nonprep, 32, 34
    Rhodes Scholars, 48
    police, 50
    school administrators, 51, 153
Jung's original, 30
letter identification of, 30
letter placement, dominance and, 14
marriage and, 123–130
of medical students, 159
most
  independent, 111
  intelligent, 66
occurrence of, unequal, 182
opposites and, 27, 119
See also individually listed (letter-designated) types; Jung, Carl G.; Opposites; Preferences; Self-selection ratio (SSR)
Type Table, 29
  characteristics of areas in, 30
  defined, 27
  divisions, 28–29
  full-size, 208–209
  incidence frequencies in, 30
  letter combinations in, 30
  relationships in
    between type and
      education, 31, 32, 34, 35, 36, 37, 38, 39
      sex, 31, 32, 34, 35, 36, 37, 38, 39
    by proximity, 28, 29, 51, 55, 67, 74

SSRs in, 40
See also Type(s), incidences of
   among

Unconscious
   of children, 131–132, 133, 134,
      135
   intuition and, 2, 57, 59, 131
   sensing and, 59
   shadow and, 84–85, 128

van der Hoop, J. H., views on
   auxiliary process, 19
   extraverted
      feeling types, 93

intuitives, 108
   sensing types, 101
introverted
   intuitives, 110–111
   sensing types, 103
type development, 168
Vernon, P. E., on personality
   classifications, 6
von Fange, E. A., on type and occupation, 71, 153

Wechsler test, 143
Wilson, Woodrow, introverted
   thinking of, 53, 89